The Prophet Who Teacheth Lies

Alexander Tibekizis

Copyright © 2023 Alexander Tibekizis
All Rights Reserved.
No Part of this book may be produced, stored in a retrieval system, or transmitted by any means without the written permission of the author.

ISBN: 978-1-916770-88-1

Dedication

To the humble and "submissive to the divine will," who are "persecuted for righteousness' sake;" sometimes, even persecuted in the so-called name of the Lord.

Table of Contents

Dedication	iii
Author's Note	v
Preface	vii
Chapter '0': Preparation	1
Chapter 1: "We Know"	3
Chapter 2: Believing - Uniting	16
Chapter 3: Intellectual Gymnastics	31
Chapter 4: Literal Godsend	46
Chapter 5: Answers to Prayers	49
Chapter 6: Standing Before God	52
Chapter 7: Standing for Truth	61
Afterward	66
Appendix 1	70
Appendix 2	73
Appendix 3	77

Author's Note

In the Declaration of Independence, the founders did not provide footnotes, references, or document and video links for every accusation they made of King George III. These were common knowledge to the perpetrator King George, the parliament elites, and the colonists who had suffered from these abuses. Similarly, the abuses and persecutions described herein are *prima facie* to those who experienced them. Nevertheless, references provided throughout the book offer useful jumping points for deeper study and validation. For those for whom the abuses and lies described herein are a surprise, or are not yet convinced of them, the author encourages them to take steps as described in chapter 0 and the afterward of this book.

The Light of Christ is given to all men such that they may recognize good and evil and choose the good. As we choose good over evil, our strength in recognizing and following that light increases.[1] Nevertheless, competing voices of the world, even religious authority, often compete with that light. With nearly every voice claiming a right to good and goodness, many become confused about where light ends and darkness begins. Martin Luther testified, "the highest worship of God is **to ascribe to him truth**, righteousness, and whatever qualities we must ascribe to one in whom we believe."[2] In that vein, this book serves as a case in point for any follower of God, illustrating what He expects of us when competing dogmas, even from the most trusted voices, entice us away from **truth**.

---

[1] A meaningful 19-page treatise on this topic is available here: https://joelskousen.com/the-still-small-voice-of-conscience
[2] "Concerning Christian Liberty; with Letter of Martin Luther to Pope Leo X", *Project Gutenberg* https://www.gutenberg.org/cache/epub/1911/pg1911-images.html

That being said, the intent of this book is to inspire hope in members of the Church of Jesus Christ of Latter-Day Saints who have felt abandoned or even betrayed by their leaders. Some recognize that President Russel M. Nelson promoted not only a lie, but an injurious action that has injured, debilitated, or killed millions of people, driving up infertility rates, and dramatically increasing stillborn births, miscarriages, and premature death. In this realization, some feel they can no longer be members of a church that espouses so blindly such blatant lies. To those, this book is a call to stay. President Nelson is called of God and appointed as a prophet. President Nelson also taught lies. The bottom line is that Christ is still in charge. Stay with the Lord's church, His people, and the covenants you have made with the Lord. This book is meant to share why it makes sense to stay.

Some believe President Nelson's direction is infallible. They have taken the vaccine against their better judgment, despite the ever-mounting evidence of the damage it causes. They feel a responsibility to vaccinate themselves and their children as a demonstration of their loyalty to God and his prophet. Some fear they will lose their salvation if they do not follow the prophet's direction to get the vaccine. They worry it is the start of apostasy to disagree with any position President Nelson takes. This book appeals to true doctrine and scripture, to prove our loyalty is first to God, rather than man, even when that man holds a very important position in the church.

For those not in one of these groups, you may find utility in this book in seeking to understand friends or loved ones with whom you want to relate or discuss these matters.

Finally, this book witnesses the persecution and lies heaped upon mankind, including members of the Church, during this revealing chapter in history.

Preface

"For the people turneth not unto him that smiteth them, neither do they seek the Lord of hosts. Therefore, the Lord will cut off from Israel head and tail, branch and rush, in one day. **The ancient and honourable, he is the head; and the prophet that teacheth lies, he is the tail.** For the leaders of this people cause them to err; and they that are led of them are destroyed."

Isaiah 9:13-16, also 2 Nephi 19:13-16

Chapter '0': Preparation

This book assumes the reader is familiar with the abuses and usurpations of what was the plandemic of Covid-19. If not, I suggest that the reader come back to this book completing at least two items on this checklist:

Watch the *Plandemic Series* at www.plandemicseries.com, specifically, the first video "Plandemic," with Judy Mikovitz, and the second video "Indoctrination,": These provide insight into the origin and planning of the greatest power grab in history. (Total time: 1 hr 38 min).

Watch *Planet Lockdown* at https://planetlockdownfilm.com/documentary/ : Panoramic presentation on the impact and corruption of the plandemic. (Total time: 1 hr 50 min).

Read *COVID-19 and the Global Predators: We Are Prey* by Dr. Peter Breggin and Ginger Breggin.

"It discloses for the first time the actual blueprint and master plan that was ten years in the making by global predators before the pandemic: a plan to reorganize the world in the name of public health." https://www.weare theprey.com/product/covid-19-and-the-global-predators-we-are-the-prey/ (690 pages).

Read *Lies My Gov't Told Me* by Dr. Robert Malone. Lies My Gov't Told Me: And the Better Future Coming • Children's Health Defense (childrenshealthdefense.org); https://www.amazon.com/dp/151077324X?linkCode=ogi&th=1&psc=1&tag=sofferscom1-20

: Wide range of scientists, medics, and other professionals "breaking down the lies about COVID-19 and shedding light on why we came to believe them." (480 pgs).

Watch *Doctors Speaking Out Against the Narrative are being Suspended and Attacked.* https://drtrozzi.org/2023/01/11/ca-persecution-of-ethical-drs-draws-international-attention/ : Example of repercussions and impact of COVID corruption on current medicine. (1 hr 18 min).

Listen to podcast episode—Situation Update (about June 6th 2021): "Mike Adams' covid vaccine message to family and friends… what you aren't being told by the establishment" https://www.brighteon.com/2495a88b-90ad-4411-9171-faef76358dbc (1 hr 47 min): One scientist's appeal early on to his own family, expressing his point of view for avoiding the vaccine. An example of information that was already known within months of vaccine release. (1 hr 47 min).

Watch *The Highwire* **Episode 319 "Awakening".** A good summary episode showing corruption behind the covid-19 vaccine, the damage it causes, and the good science that was suppressed to ensure no treatment could compete with the vaccine. https://thehighwire.com/ark-videos/awakening/ (2hr 20 min).

Chapter 1: "We Know"

On Jan 19th, 2021, hours before President Biden was inaugurated president of the United States the next day, President Russell M. Nelson (RMN) posted on his Twitter and other social media accounts that he and other Church leaders received their first vaccination shot for covid-19. He referred to the shot as a "literal Godsend."[3]

The First Presidency instructed Church members in an official statement to "help quell the pandemic by safeguarding themselves and others through immunization."[4] RMN also said that getting the vaccine was a part of their "personal efforts to be good global citizens in helping to eliminate COVID-19 from the world."

At this point in time, those that were aware of the falsehoods surrounding covid-19 could already see the foolishness of rushing to get this vaccine. However, as the months wore on, harmful side effects began to mount from the uptake of the vaccine. As study after study showed that masks were either ineffective or increased individual vulnerability to disease, this writer was hopeful that the Church's policy would soon ease in its pursuit to apply covid-19 measures that were making the disease worse. However, such hopes were crushed a few months later as the First Presidency doubled down on its position.

On August 12th, 2021, the First Presidency, comprising of President Russell M. Nelson, 1st Counselor Dallin H. Oaks, and 2nd counselor Henry B. Eyring, signed and issued a letter worldwide to convince all members of the Church that they should take the covid-19 jab, otherwise referenced as *the* vaccine. They stated:

---
[3] https://twitter.com/NelsonRussellM/status/1351575425756012546
[4] https://newsroom.churchofjesuschrist.org/article/church-leaders-covid-19-vaccine

Dear Brothers and Sisters: We find ourselves fighting a war against the ravages of COVID-19 and its variants, an unrelenting pandemic. We want to do all we can to limit the spread of these viruses. We know that protection from the diseases they cause can only be achieved by immunizing a very high percentage of the population. To limit exposure to these viruses, we urge the use of face masks in public meetings whenever social distancing is not possible. To provide personal protection from such severe infections, we urge individuals to be vaccinated. Available vaccines have proven to be both safe and effective. We can win this war if everyone will follow the wise and thoughtful recommendations of medical experts and government leaders. Please know of our sincere love and great concern for all of God's children.

The First Presidency

Russell M. Nelson, Dallin H. Oaks, Henry B. Eyring

This statement was a complete lie, from the first sentence to the last. By issuing this letter, these prophets, in particular President Nelson, unequivocally, publicly, and unabashedly became a prophet teaching lies. He led many to err. The destruction left in that wake has already been significant, with more yet to come.

Part of this destruction was the annihilation of trust and brotherly love among many members of the Church. Seemingly overnight, the Church became a model of Germany in the early 30s. Party members proudly demonstrated loyalty to their führer with unceasing praises and declarations of his sagacity, this time by wearing face masks instead of armbands, and members who would not join in the falsehoods fell suddenly suspect as non-party members and regarded by many as apostates.[5] Family members were told they could not be members of the church if they didn't accept the prophet's words as doctrine.

---

[5] "Some Latter-day Saints have accused those who promote anti-vaccine rhetoric of apostasy, a term that is associated with wickedness and describes when individuals turn away from church principles," Sophia Eppolito, Salt Lake City, Associated Press. https://news.yahoo.com/mormon-vaccine-push-ratchets-dividing-041316188.html, 30 Aug 2021.

Pulling apart the First Presidency's statement sentence by sentence reveals the falsehood of each statement:

Dear Brothers and Sisters: We find ourselves fighting a war against the ravages of COVID-19 and its variants, an unrelenting pandemic.

This sentence is a lie. It was not an unrelenting pandemic.[6] Real mortality was equal to the seasonal flu. An epidemiological assessment showed covid mortality for ages 0-59 was only 0.035%. For 0-19 the percentage was only 0.0003%. Even at the highest ratio measured for 60-69 it was only 0.501%. This is with 86% of the US population under the age of 60.[7] Even these percentages are inflated as hospitals and governments attributed enormous quantities of deaths from other causes to covid, thus making records inflate covid death numbers to make it appear that covid-19 was an emergency.[8] On top of that, most that died from covid had an average of 2.6 comorbidities; in other words, with or without covid, they were likely going to die at or near the same time. Death resulting only from covid were few and hard to

---

[6] Dr. Charles Hoffe summed this up: "This pandemic, it is very clear that the forces of evil on this planet have been preparing for this for a long time. But this crisis that they created, with this virus that, even at its very worst, was no more dangerous than the flu, but they created a massive crisis in order to be able to impose what they called 'safety', … all of the restrictions were to keep us 'safe' from this 'terrible danger' that was no worse than the flu. But what this has really done, this has been a moral integrity test. This entire pandemic at every level, with doctors, with health regulators, with the media, with our elected officials, with people in the community, covid-19 has been a moral integrity test" ("Doctors Speaking Out Against the Narrative are being Suspended and Attacked" 56:24-57:25, CHD Europe, Dr. Mark Trozzi, https://drtrozzi.org/2023/01/11/ca-persecution-of-ethical-drs-draws-international-attention/ , 11 Jan 2023z).

[7] "A Closer Look At the Covid Mortality Rate", Ian Miller, Brownstone Institute, A Closer Look at the Covid Mortality Rate ★ Brownstone Institute, 23 Oct 2022.

[8] "In normal times, medical error would account for more than 5000 deaths per *week*. But since early 2020, medical error hasn't killed a single person, if we rely upon news stories and the CDC. It's all COVID all the time. In normal times, medical errors were the bane of hospital legal departments, but not during the pandemic. Anomalous deaths of people who had at some point tested positive for COVID were not scrutinized, investigated, debated, or litigated over—and there were no autopsies. Everything was automatically a COVID death. And even if we were to accept every single one of those as having been caused by COVID, the sats would remain: *Almost all patients whose deaths were attributed to COVID-19 were elderly people already struggling with more than two fatal illnesses.*" Gavin de Becker, "Children on the Back of a Mad Elephant" in *Lies My Gov't Told Me: And the Better Future Coming*, Robert M. Malone, p. 58-59. Skyhorse Publishing 2022. Kindle.

find. In Italy, where the number of cases caused great alarm for the rest of the world, over 97% of "covid deaths" had comorbidities.[9] Covid itself was very manageable unless exacerbated by injurious lung rupturing respirator treatments or kidney killing remdesivir.

We want to do all we can to limit the spread of these viruses.

This is not true. Masking policies were shown to increase the spread of illness. If they wanted to do all they could to limit the spread, they would have encouraged Vitamin D[10] uptake and the protocols that were helping people, such as Ivermectin,[11] Budesonide,[12] and Hydroxychloroquine.[13] If they truly wanted to do *all* they could, why didn't they recommend what was working?

*We **know** that protection from the diseases they cause can **only** be achieved by immunizing a very high percentage of the population. (emphasis added)*

This is perhaps the greatest lie of all because of on how many levels it is a lie. First, there was no way anyone could know that this was the *only* way to get protection from the disease. But why not? Because there was no testing to prove that protection could be acquired through

---

[9] https://www.statista.com/statistics/1110906/comorbidities-in-covid-19-deceased-patients-in-italy/ ; see also, Characteristics of SARS-CoV-2 patients dying in Italy Report based on available data on October 5th, 2021, https://www.epicentro.iss.it/en/coronavirus/bollettino/Report-COVID-2019_5_october_2021.pdf , p.3.

[10] "Evidence from observational studies is accumulating, suggesting that the majority of deaths due to SARS-CoV-2 infections are statistically attributable to vitamin D insufficiency and could potentially be prevented by vitamin D supplementation" Hermann Brenner, Ben Schottker, https://pubmed.ncbi.nlm.nih.gov/33260798/, 27 Nov 2020.

[11] "These data show that ivermectin is effectively a "miracle drug" against COVID-19. The magnitude of the effect is similar to its Nobel prize-worthy historical impacts against parasitic disease across many parts of the globe." From "Testimony of Pierre Kory, MD, Homeland Security Committee Meeting: Focus on Early Treatment of COVID-19, December 8, 2020", https://www.hsgac.senate.gov/imo/media/doc/Testimony-Kory-2020-12-08.pdf, 8 Dec 2020. See also "Dr. Peter McCullough's Interview on "American Thought Leaders – The Epoch Times" https://youtu.be/CA-Yhq1GXhk .

[12] https://budesonideworks.com/, https://www.behindthecurtaintv.com/ ; Dr. Richard Bartlett saw dramatic cure rates as early as July 2020, see interview here: https://americacanwetalk.org/panic-porn-dr-richard-bartlett-independence-day-brilliance-7-2-20/ (minutes 7:40-38:45).

the vaccine and absolutely no scientific literature on what percentage of the population is required to be vaccinated for "immunity." In addition, RMN's statement completely ignores natural immunity, which a person acquires when they fight off the disease and either recover or are infected and never experience symptoms. Furthermore, this statement completely ignored any therapeutic efforts that could be made to protect oneself from the disease, either that currently existed or that could exist in the future.

Sadly, by this statement, they managed to exclude the power of God himself as a source of protection from the disease. Their message: Trust in the arm of man and the pharmaceutical companies—companies already sued and convicted for billions for lying about other drugs[14]—and we will all get through this!

To claim that a vaccine was the one and only solution was the greatest false and arrogant sales point that a vaccine company could ever hope to make. The only way the First Presidency could know such a statement to be true would have been through divine revelation, and this statement took advantage of their position as "prophets, seers, and revelators" to convince Church members that it was true. Indeed, it was exactly because they were prophets that many believed this sales point for which there was no evidence. The fact that the prophet said he *knew* the vaccine was the only way was evidence to them that indeed God had talked to him, because this statement could only be true if God had done so. Yet this was teaching a lie. A lie from the vaccine companies and public health officials to convince people to take a minimally tested injection, and even when tested, hiding from the public the many health problems experienced in those in the trials.[15]

---

[14] "The four major companies who are making COVID vaccines are/have either: Never brought a vaccine to market before COVID (Moderna and Johnson & Johnson). Are serial felons (Pfizer, and AstraZeneca). Are both (Johnson & Johnson)" from "18 Reasons I Won't Be Getting a COVID Vaccine", Christian Elliot, https://childrenshealthdefense.org/defender/reasons-not-getting-covid-vaccine/, 15 April 2021.

[15] "CHD Says Pfizer Clinical Trial Data Contradicts 'Safe and Effective' Government/Industry Mantra", Children's Health Defense, https://childrenshealthdefense.org/press-release/chd-says-pfizer-clinical-trial-data-contradicts-safe-and-effective/, 3 March 2022. See also "CNN: Vaccine Advisors 'Angry,' 'Disappointed' Moderna, FDA and CDC Hid Data on COVID

The pharmaceutical companies had to maintain the tenet that there was no other way to get protection from the disease in order to acquire emergency use authorization in the United States.[16] The First Presidency went to bat for them, convincing as many as they could that the very situation existed which would allow the distribution of products that would have never been lawful if therapeutic treatments to covid were acknowledged.[17]

This statement implies divine revelation, implies acting as the Lord's mouthpiece because they left no room for speculation; they *knew*, when there was no other way to know other than God himself. Knowing that the Lord had not actually given them this *knowledge*, making such a statement as his mouthpiece was a form of taking the Lord's name in vain.[18]

> *To limit exposure to these viruses, we urge the use of face masks in public meetings whenever social distancing is not possible.*

Boosters", Children's Health Defense, https://childrenshealthdefense.org/defender/cnn-moderna-fda-cdc-covid-boosters/, 12 Jan 2023.

[16]"An EUA can only be granted when no adequate, approved, available alternatives exist", Yale Medicine, https://www.yalemedicine.org/news/what-does-eua-mean, 7 Mar 2022). See also the FDA: "emergency use authorization is appropriate, FDA may authorize unapproved medical products or unapproved uses of approved medical products to be used in an emergency to diagnose, treat, or prevent serious or life-threatening diseases or conditions caused by CBRN threat agents when certain criteria are met, including there are no adequate, approved, and available alternatives" ("Emergency Use Authorization", FDA, https://www.fda.gov/emergency-preparedness-and-response/mcm-legal-regulatory-and-policy-framework/emergency-use-authorization, accessed 23 Jan 2023).

[17]"They engineered new legislation in Jan 2017, ... they passed in Congress, the emergency use authority, so that they could bypass the FDA and get a red stamp without proving safety or efficacy if a drug was urgently needed, or a vaccine was urgently needed; and the caveat was that if they had a safe and effective drug [to respond to the emergency], they couldn't rush through a drug or vaccine. So, Bill Gates had already bet billions on it, Moderna had been working on this for three years, this did not start during Covid-19. Three years beforehand, they were tooling up for this." Dr. Peter Breggin, ACWT Interview 20 April 2021 https://americacanwetalk.org/dr-peter-breggin-acwt-interview-4-20-21/ (10:50-12:10). See also Peter and Ginger Breggin's book *COVID-19 and the Global Predators: We are the Prey*, https://www.weretheprey.com/product/covid-19-and-the-global-predators-we-are-the-prey/

[18]This is reminiscent of Jeremiah's words, "I have not sent these prophets, yet they ran: I have not spoken to them, yet they prophesied" (Jer 23:21).

To promote face masks as a protection from these viruses is a complete sham.[19] Another lie. Even Fauci stated that they could not provide protection from respiratory viruses.[20] The masks were a form of psychological manipulation to make people believe there was a pandemic emergency, to make obvious who was not compliant with the state's lies (just like party arm bands), and a method of perpetuating disease and making more people sick.[21] The First Presidency's unity with the pharmaceutical establishment to promote this lie is a key indicator of how aligned with political theater rather than health interests these leaders were.

To provide personal protection from such severe infections, we urge individuals to be vaccinated.

These injections were never tested against severe infections. Their

---

[19] Study: "These findings indicate that countries with high levels of mask compliance did not perform better than those with low mask usage" ("Correlation Between Mask Compliance and COVID-19 Outcomes in Europe", Spira B (April 19, 2022) Correlation Between Mask Compliance and COVID-19 Outcomes in Europe. Cureus 14(4): e24268. doi:10.7759/cureus.24268). https://www.ncbi.nlm.nih.gov/pmc/articles/PMC9123350/

[20] "In an email to former Health and Human Services Secretary Sylvia Burwell on February 5, 2020—as concerns over the new Coronavirus in China were just starting to make their way to the United States—Fauci assured her that wearing a mask was unnecessary. 'Masks are really for infected people to prevent them from spreading infection to people who are not infected rather than protecting uninfected people from acquiring infection,' he wrote. 'The typical mask you buy in the drug store is not really effective at keeping out virus, which is small enough to pass through the material'" ("Can We Finally Admit That Mask-Wearing Was Pointless?", MacIver Institute, https://www.maciverinstitute.com/2021/06/can-we-finally-admit-that-mask-wearing-was-pointless/, 4 Jun 2021).

[21] "There is increasing evidence that cloth masks not only may be ineffective against stopping coronavirus transmission, but that they may actually increase the spread of the virus, as well as worsening other health conditions" ("CDC Admits: No Conclusive Evidence Cloth Masks Work Against COVID", Raven Clabough, The New American, https://thenewamerican.com/cdc-admits-no-conclusive-evidence-cloth-masks-work-against-covid/, 29 Oct 2020). Also summary of lab report after masks were sent to a lab for analysis "Half of the masks were contaminated with one or more strains of pneumonia-causing bacteria. One-third were contaminated with one or more strains of meningitis-causing bacteria. One-third were contaminated with dangerous, antibiotic-resistant bacterial pathogens. In addition, less dangerous pathogens were identified, including pathogens that can cause fever, ulcers, acne, yeast infections, strep throat, periodontal disease, Rocky Mountain Spotted Fever, and more" ("Dangerous Pathogens found on Children's Face Masks", Jennifer Carera, Rational Ground, https://rationalground.com/dangerous-pathogens-found-on-childrens-face-masks/, 16 June 2021).

testing protocols were only compared against mild symptoms.[22] Once again, the First Presidency makes reference to knowledge that no other human on the planet had, that these could protect from severe infections. Certainly, they were not the only ones promoting this talking point. President Biden and his allied media also harped on this same point, but likewise without proof. The truth has proved otherwise, with the vaccinated more prone to hospitalization and illness.[23] As "mouthpieces of the Lord," this lie, made as an official announcement, under the capacity of leaders of the Church, was allowed to perpetuate as if with the strength of being spoken by the Lord himself. Once again, to promote a lie, under the guise and role of promulgators of divine knowledge, is to take the Lord's name in vain.

Available vaccines have proven to be both safe and effective.

Once again – a LIE. A lie perpetuated by the government and vaccine makers. There was no way these could be *proven* safe and effective as not enough time had passed from development to actually test them for safety and efficacy. That is *why* they had to be issued under emergency use authorization (EUA) *because* it was *impossible* to prove safety in such a short period of time. If they were really *proven* to be safe and effective, there would not have been any need for EUA.

The results have proven how enormously ineffective and unsafe these vaccines were. Florida retracted its recommendation for youth to take the vaccine, as youth who take the vaccine are 84% more likely

---

[22] "Three of the vaccine protocols—Moderna, Pfizer, and AstraZeneca—do not require that their vaccine prevent serious disease only that they prevent moderate symptoms which may be as mild as cough, or headache" (Covid-19 Vaccine Protocols Reveal That Trials Are Designed To Succeed", William A Haseltine, Forbes, https://www.forbes.com/sites/williamhaseltine/2020/09/23/covid-19-vaccine-protocols-reveal-that-trials-are-designed-to-succeed/?sh=4a055dc35247, 23 Sep 2020).

[23] "DATA REVEALS HIGHER COVID RATE IN THE VACCINATED", The Highwire, https://thehighwire.com/videos/data-reveals-higher-covid-rate-in-the-vaccinated/?fbclid=IwAR3Sy5FIUIplN_MpwnXNWISpwAx8FKLqQZ8N5UQSv0PmtzRRxoWZM8HswI0, 27 Jan 2022 (excerpt from Episode 252).

to suffer cardiac problems.[24] The working population has seen more death in 2021 than during the Vietnam war. The stillbirth rate has increased over 40-sigma in some hospitals (40 standard deviations from the mean!) since the vaccines were rolled out.[25] These numbers didn't happen in 2020 when the "pandemic" was raging unbridled, with no vaccines available. It occurred in 2021 when the vaccine came out and when so many got injected. Actors collapsing on stage, athletes dying during games and sporting events,[26] people dying with blood clots, and embalmers finding 75% of dead bodies with blood clots instead of 5-7% in the pre-covid-vaccine era. Hundreds of thousands died or received permanent injury from the vaccine, having taken it because they were told it was safe. Some of these were Church members. Believing their prophet was speaking the word of the Lord, many Church members believed the shot was safe and effective even though there was no proof to substantiate such a claim.

We can win this war if everyone will follow the wise and thoughtful recommendations of medical experts and government leaders.

Once again, acting like covid waged "war," encouraged the state of fear and panic that allowed people to accept the theft of their

---

[24] "EXCLUSIVE: Dr. Joseph Ladapo on Why He's Not Recommending mRNA COVID Vaccines for Healthy, Young Men—'People Deserve Honesty'", Jan Jekielek, The Epoch Times, https://www.theepochtimes.com/exclusive-dr-joseph-ladapo-on-why-hes-not-recommending-mrna-covid-vaccines-for-healthy-young-men-people-deserve-honesty_4808208.html?utm_source=ai&utm_medium=search, 20 Oct 2022.

[25] Dr. James A. Thorp, MD, OBGYN "I've seen death and destruction like I have never seen before …. 1200 fold increases in menstrual abnormalities. Then when we get into pregnancy, we're looking at a substantial increase in miscarriages and birth defects, a substantial risk of fetal cardiac arrhythmia, fetal cardiac malformations, significant fetal growth slowing, significant reduction in amniotic fluid, fetal cardiac arrests … the vaccine causes a significant inflammatory effect." Dr. Jim Thorp: "Now let's go to 2021, look at the still birth rate…this is horrifying…that sigma that you're looking at is 40 plus sigma. Standard Deviation. Let that sink in" ("World Premiere: Died Suddenly" 56:40-59:16, Stew Peters Network, https://rumble.com/v1wac7i-world-premier-died-suddenly.html, 21 Nov 2022).

[26] "Healthy athletes are still inexplicably collapsing", The Highwire, https://thehighwire.com/videos/healthy-athletes-are-still-inexplicably-collapsing/ 21 Jan 2022. This clip also documents how insurance companies are seeing a 200-year catastrophe in the all-cause mortality of working-age adults 18-49 with the influence of the vaccine.

rights and freedoms while irrationally injecting themselves and their children with a concoction; the contents, hazards, and consequences of which, the doctors administering them were not fully aware. These "recommendations" were not recommendations but tyrannical, mean, and unlawful mandates.[27] They were the very opposite of thoughtful, in the sense of politeness or consideration of another's welfare. In many parts of the world, including the United States, these *mandates* caused many to submit, or be persecuted with the loss of their jobs and exclusion from everyday activities and public locations. In addition to *unthoughtful* recommendations, these policies were unwise. Is it wise to blanket an entire population at the same time with an experimental product? Is it wise to require useless masks on everyone to ensure they can maximize their bacterial load throughout the day? These were not wise and thoughtful recommendations, and to paint them as so was simply another lie. By declaring a war against covid, the First Presidency actually fomented the war of the elites against the populace, their weapons: the "recommendations" and "mandates" that caused unprecedented socio-economic pain and disruption.

Please know of our sincere love and great concern for all of God's children.

In 2021, this writer thought that perhaps this was the only true statement of the First Presidency letter.

Perhaps the First Presidency really did love us.

Since then, however, their actions have proven that this is also a lie. They prefer their power and prestige and their status among the nations far more than concern they have for the well-being of God's children. If they truly had concern for God's children they would

---

[27] One example of mandates observed in medical care: "We now see government-dictated medical care at its worst in our history since the federal government *mandated* these ineffective and dangerous treatments for COVID-19, and then *created financial incentives* for hospitals and doctors to use only those "approved" (and paid for) approaches." "Biden's Bounty On Your Life: Hospitals' Incentive Payments for COVID-19," Elizabeth Lee Vliet, M.D. and Ali Shultz, J.D., AAPS (Association of American Physicians and Surgeons), https://aapsonline.org/bidens-bounty-on-your-life-hospitals-incentive-payments-for-covid-19/, 17 Nov 2021.

not have promoted policies that increased pharmaceutical murder.[28] They continued promoting lies, even as evidence continued to mount that there were other, much more effective and safe ways to treat this problem.[29] They continued their mantra that only the vaccine was the answer. They made the vaccine a requirement for both young and old to serve missions outside their home country. They preferred to pursue their quid-pro-quo agenda with the rulers of the earth (see the next chapter), even if it meant some who believed their lies had to be injured or killed in the process.

Perhaps the First Presidency has other concerns they deem are of greater concern than God's children, in which case they could potentially still have great love and concern for them, however misguided their actions in expressing this love may be. It is the opinion of this writer however that the lying paradigm that permeated this letter was maintained through this last sentence as well. This sentence served as a disarming blow and misdirection of motive. It made the letter appear that it was written with the sole concern of God's children in mind, when actually, as we will see in the next chapter, curing favor with the world's elite was their advertised motive to this very elite.

A general authority, while speaking to Church leaders, commented that many who resisted taking the vaccine, believe they are correct because RMN did not say, "thus saith the Lord." This is a ridiculous attempt to create a straw man for the reasons some Church members chose not to follow RMN on this instruction. As if all the lies manifested above were of no consequence. However, what this argument does demonstrate, is that leaders of the Church EXPECTED Church members to take this recommendation as coming from the Lord himself.[30] They argue RMN did not need to say "thus

---

[28]See "Data Proves US Pharmacies Poisoned The World". Ben Armstrong, The New American. https://thenewamerican.com/data-proves-us-pharmacies-poisoned-the-world/ , 12 Jan 2023.
[29]See quote from Catherine Austin Fitts in footnote 101.
[30]Another example is Elder Allen D. Haynie's talk from the April 2023 General Conference. https://www.churchofjesuschrist.org/study/general-conference/2023/04/16haynie?lang=eng. From the perspective Haynie teaches, there is no room to recognize the lies RMN was teaching. The only option from this point of view would have been to take the vaccine.

saith the Lord" for people to respect this instruction as coming from the Lord. Indeed, when a prophet is acting as God's mouthpiece this is a correct sentiment, but a man serving in the position of president of the Church also has times when he can be acting as a man. The prophet Joseph Smith taught that a prophet is a prophet only when he is acting as such.[31]

Isaiah 9: 13-16 states *"For the people turneth not unto him that smiteth them, neither do they seek the Lord of hosts. Therefore, the Lord will cut off from Israel head and tail, branch and rush, in one day. The ancient and honourable, he is the head; and* **the prophet that teacheth lies**, *he is the tail.* **For the leaders of this people cause them to err; and they that are led of them are destroyed**.*"* *(also quoted in 2 Ne 19: 13-16).*

President Nelson, currently matches the description of a prophet that teaches lies. Some may protest on behalf of his ignorance. "But he wasn't lying! He thought all he said was true." Indeed, as difficult as it may seem that someone so well-versed in medicine could be blind to these lies, perhaps he really believed them. In that case, he was teaching someone else's lie. In either case, he was a prophet teaching a well-formulated set of lies.

In summary, the August 2021 statement is sufficient to establish that the First Presidency was promoting a solution to the 'pandemic' based on lies. These lies were particularly effective in deceiving those who trusted in the arm of flesh and in man's wisdom, and those that "follow the prophet" without seeking a personal witness of the truth.

---

[31] "It would seem that the Prophet spent half his time trying to convince the slow and sludgy people who had a little faith that God was indeed with him and with them; and that he spent the other half alerting the Saints that a prophet is a prophet only when he is acting as such, which means when he is inspired of God. The rest of the time, he is a mere mortal—has opinions, makes mistakes, and in a general way of speaking has to put his pants on one leg at a time as every other man does" (*Joseph Smith Lecture 2: Joseph's Personality and Character*), Truman G. Madsen, 22 Aug 1978. https://speeches.byu.edu/talks/truman-g-madsen/joseph-smiths-personality-and-character/

A personal note: As the days of summer of 2021 wore on, and the harmful effects of the vaccine combined with the lies surrounding it became more apparent, this writer took hope that by general conference the Church's stance on Covid-19 measures would relax with regard to the vaccine. I thought it was surely a short time before the error of the vaccine, along with the faults of recommendations to take it, were made plain. Surely, I thought, requirements and recommendations to take it for missionaries and various temple workers, would be rescinded. To my shock and amazement, on 12 August 2021, not only was a retracement not forthcoming, the First Presidency doubled down, making claims the vaccine was safe and effective. The shock could not leave my mind until I analyzed the First Presidency letter sentence by sentence a few days later, then I understood what was shocking to me about it; I discovered every single sentence was a lie. Until sorting this out for myself and analyzing each sentence one at a time, I did not realize how blatant the lies were. Appendix 2 is what I wrote in early September 2021 as I sorted this out. This early assessment within days of the First Presidency letter acts as another summary and witness of evidence that was already known at the time.

Chapter 2: Believing - Uniting

The Covid jab, as documented in *The Real Anthony Fauci* by David Kennedy, Jr, was the most recent in a long line of many years where Fauci and the pharmaceutical companies participated cooperatively to make money at the mortal expense of the population. This latest scheme also provided money-making opportunities from several avenues for the Fauci club, and was done in such a way as to dull the moral senses of the medical profession that would need to implement the money-making scheme at the ground level. How was morality blurred? With money, of course![32]

Remdesivir, pulled from the shelves for causing kidney failure, was made standard of care by Fauci's NIH and sold for $3,000 a course.[33] When prescribed, hospitals would get an additional rebate from the government for 20% of the entire cost of the hospital stay of the individual receiving the Remdesivir prescription, which was the tip of the iceberg; hospitals were paid a range of $166,00-$477,0000 more by the government in perverse covid treatment incentives which "turned hospitals and medical staffs into 'bounty hunters,' and Covid patients into 'virtual prisoners'."[34] The "vaccine," promulgated as protection

---

[32] "[The devil] tempts men to make small sacrifices of their principles in order to obtain wealth, and the small compromises eventually lead to greater ones. This was one of the major factors in the apostasy of Christ's church because riches drew men away from their dependency on God." Ogden Kraut, *Trusting In the Arm of Flesh*, p. 171. Pioneer Publishing. http://ogdenkraut.com/?page_id=128

[33] "Remdesivir Priced At More Than $3,100 For A Course of Treatment", Sydney Lupkin, NPR, https://www.npr.org/sections/health-shots/2020/06/29/884648842/remdesivir-priced-at-more-than-3-100-for-a-course-of-treatment. 29 June 2020.

[34] Quoted from Dr. Elizabeth Lee Vliet and Ali Shultz, JD, "who wrote a widely distributed op-ed in late 2021 for the Association of American Physicians and Surgeons (AAPS)". "How Billions in COVID Stimulus Funds Led Hospitals to Prioritize 'Treatments' That Killed, Rather Than Cured, Patients," Children's Health Defense Team, The Defender, https://

from Covid and a "protection to others," was shown not only to have no effect on reducing transmission but made those with the vaccine more likely to suffer from Covid, with a high incidence of serious and irreparable injury, including death.[35] Nevertheless, after receiving billions from American taxpayers to develop a 'vaccine,' the vaccine makers, made bumper crop profits dwarfing their entire history. With no agreement to buy at wholesale, the U.S. paid retail for the vaccines. Pfizer alone stood to make over $36 billion on jabs for kids alone.[36] Governments the world over made vaccine purchase and uptake the focus of their agenda.

Both the vaccine manufacturers and the medical bureaucracy in the United States were aware that the vaccine was not proven to do all they promised. Evidence surfaced that the companies masked dangerous side effects in the approval process. In 2022 Deborah Birx admitted publicly that they oversold the effectiveness of the vaccine.[37] Yet, no restraint was permitted in pushing for mandates to uptake the vaccine by governments throughout the world.

childrenshealthdefense.org/defender/billions-covid-stimulus-hospitals-treatments-killed-patients/, 24 Jan 2022. Also, see the incredible op-ed here: https://aapsonline.org/bidens-bounty-on-your-life-hospitals-incentive-payments-for-covid-19/ (AAPS, "Biden's Bounty on Your Life: Hospitals' Incentive Payments for COVID-19", 17 Nov 2021).

[35] Many sources of many months documenting this, but Robert Malone summed it up nicely: "The Cleveland Clinic report and data from all over the world have now demonstrated that those that receive these multiple jabs, including the booster, have had this problem that I predicted in sworn testimony in the senate in Texas, immune imprinting, and the shifting of immune responses that is making those that receive these products more likely to be hospitalized or die, and more likely to get infected with significant symptoms. We now clearly have a pandemic, if you want to call it that, of the vaccinated, not the unvaccinated, consequent to the repeated inoculations." From "Dr. Robert Malone: FDA Advisors Disappointed in Data of Pandemic of the Vaccinated". Bannon War Room. https://rumble.com/v24ysm4-dr.-robert-malone-fda-advisors-disappointed-in-data-of-pandemic-of-the-vacc.html, 11 Jan 2023.

[36] "This year, Pfizer has banked on selling 115 million **pediatric** doses to the U.S. government and expects to earn $36 billion in vaccine revenue. Congress is so in the pocket of Big Pharma that it's against the law for our government to negotiate bulk pricing for drugs, meaning taxpayers must pay retail" (emphasis added). *Lies My Gov't Told Me: And the Better Future Coming*, Robert M. Malone, p. 112. Skyhorse Publishing 2022. Kindle. From the original article by Leonard C. Goodman in the *Chicago Reader*, 24 Nov 2021, "Vaxxing Our Kids: Why I'm Not Rushing to Get My Six-Year-Old the COVID-19 Vaccine".

[37] Birx: "I knew these vaccines were not going to protect against infection. And I think we overplayed the vaccines", Fox News, 22 July 2022, https://www.foxnews.com/media/dr-deborah-birx-knew-covid-vaccines-not-protect-against-infection.

In Canada, truckers were not allowed to cross the U.S-Canada border without having the vaccine (prompting one of the most historic demonstrations for freedom in modern history with the trucker's convoy).[38] In the United States, President Biden attempted to require all companies over 100 employees doing business with the government to require their employees to get the vaccine. In Europe and Israel, Covid passports were uploaded through phone apps to prove vaccination before entering theaters, restaurants, and public transportation. Members of the U.S. military were required to take the shot and some threatened with court martial if they refused.

Additionally, many companies, wanting either to pad their opportunities with the government or, taken in by all the propaganda, followed the behest of government officials to pressure an increased uptake of the vaccine. Honeywell, Xero Shoes, Delta Airlines, Southwest Airlines, United Airlines, Walmart, Netflix, Walt Disney and many others, made it a policy not to hire anyone without proof of taking the jab.[39] Others, like McDonalds or the mining company Freeport McMoRan[40] hindered promotion and other career opportunities by requiring any who worked at or visited company headquarters to be vaccinated. Many hospitals required all employees to be vaccinated, prompting thousands of doctors and nurses to sacrifice their jobs rather than take the jab.[41] Other voices called for jailing people who refused the vaccine[42], or to refuse them medical care.[43] This is just

---

[38]"Truckers Make History in Canada", The Highwire with Del Bigtree, https://thehighwire.com/videos/truckers-make-history-in-canada/, 7 Feb 2022.

[39]"From McDonald's to Goldman Sachs, here are the companies mandating vaccines for all or some employees", Haley Messenger, NBC News, https://www.nbcnews.com/business/business-news/here-are-companies-mandating-vaccines-all-or-some-employees-n1275808

[40]https://me.smenet.org/webContent.cfm?webarticleid=3779

[41]"How many employees have hospitals lost to vaccine mandates? Here are the numbers so far", Dave Muoio, Fierce Healthcare, https://www.fiercehealthcare.com/hospitals/how-many-employees-have-hospitals-lost-to-vaccine-mandates-numbers-so-far, 22 Feb 2022.

[42]One example is Jacksonville Jaguars offensive lineman Uche Nwaneri called for jailing those who refused the vaccine on his twitter page, 1 Sept 2021. "Ex-NFL Player Who Called for Jailing Vaccine Resisters Dies Suddenly," The New American, 6 January 2023, https://thenewamerican.com/ex-nfl-player-who-called-for-jailing-vaccine-resisters-dies-suddenly/.

[43]For example, the situation described in Georgia and Australia by The Epoch Times "It's 2023 and Patients Are Still Being Denied Medical Treatment Because of COVID-19 Vaccines." https://www.theepochtimes.com/its-2023-and-patients-are-still-being-denied-medical-treatment-because-of-covid-19-vaccines_5244345.html.

the tip of the iceberg of the persecution against those who refused the vaccine.

The Church of Jesus Christ of Latter-Day Saints also polled all its paid employees to ask if they were vaccinated for Covid-19 or if they would be willing to do so. In the same poll, they asked if employees worked in the Utah area or outside of it. At least some temple workers were required to be vaccinated, and this author knows of at least one patriarch who was told he would not be allowed to give blessings unless he was vaccinated. Members of the tabernacle choir were required to have the jab in order to perform. Missionaries had to vaccinate to travel outside of their home countries, and masks were required to be worn worldwide in all temples.

This environment was like the Nazi rules for employment during the 1930s. In Germany it started when doctors and lawyers and journalists were not allowed to be of Jewish descent. Even if they did not know they had Jewish blood in them, if they could not prove otherwise, they would lose their jobs. One prominent journalist in Germany found out she was the granddaughter of a Jew in the process of trying to prove she was Aryan. At the time, she was a good friend of the daughter of the Ambassador of the United States to Germany. When the journalist found out she would lose her job because of her Jewish ancestry she committed suicide.[44] During the plandemic, what was in our blood also became the standard by which employment was contingent. Nearly the entire elite class, whether in business, government, media, or religion, united with those who were trading death for money, all the while hiding their own data and lying to the public.

The Book of Mormon documents a time when *the more part of the Nephites,* **"did unite with those bands of robbers, and**

---

[44]*In the Garden of Beasts,* Eric Larson, Crown Publishers, 2011. Kindle. In November 1933, Germany passed a law "that barred Jews from editing and writing for German Newspapers and required members of the domestic press to present documentation from civil and church records to prove they were 'Aryan'" (p.188-189). The withdrawal of employment opportunities for Jews, the suicide of the leading journalist Poulette as a consequence of this law, and the progression of these oppressions are well recounted in that book.

did enter into their covenants and their oaths" Helaman 6:12. What did the Gadianton robbers do? They eventually had "sole management of the government." How did they do that? They had "seduced the more part of the righteous until they had come down to **believe** in their works and partake of their **spoils**." **Believing** in their works was how the more part of the Nephites came to support them, even though they were not Gadiantons themselves. How many in our day **believed** the vaccine was actually helpful? How many **believed** that the ONLY way to stop the 'pandemic' was with the vaccine? *"We know that protection from the diseases they cause can **only** be achieved by immunizing a very high percentage of the population."* With the First Presidency's pronouncement, many came to *believe* the lie and supported it.

What covenants and oaths did the Gadianton's of our day require? What spoils did they offer for joining with them?

We saw the more part of our country and the church, especially church leaders, come to believe the lies that Covid was a pandemic,[45] that lockdown of the healthy was necessary, and that they should make every effort to make sure that the most injurious vaccine in history should be taken by everyone, all of which promoted the result of increasing death. By promoting the vaccine, "the more part of the Nephites" in our day joined "with them in their secret murders and combinations" (Helaman 6:38). RMN and many others instrumental in promoting vaccination through rules and mandates may not have

---

[45] In 2009, the WHO lowered the bar for the declaration of a pandemic by changing its definition of a pandemic, thereby making the contracts pharmaceutical companies had with Germany, France, Italy, the UK, and other countries obligatory to buy Swine Flu vaccines. These contracts could only be enforced if a pandemic was declared. This simple declaration, now made possible by a change of a few words, initiated over $ 18 billion in spending worldwide, funneling into the coffers of the vaccine makers. Doctors commented at the time "But this is not the definition of a pandemic I learned, which has to be severe, with a much higher than usual death rate." Also, "since that was no longer one of the criteria, it made it easier to declare a pandemic." For this reason, while the WHO may have called COVID-19 a pandemic, it was done so in a paradigm where most people thought 'pandemic' still meant an unusual death rate, but, it did not. See discussion and video on this topic here: "WHO exposed: How health body changed pandemic criteria to push agenda," Joel Day, Express, https://www.express.co.uk/news/world/1281081/who-world-health-organisation-coronavirus-latest-swine-flu-covid-19-europe-politics-spt, 12 May 2020.

planned the murders, but by supporting those who knew the danger of the vaccine, they joined them in promoting exactly the lies they wanted promoted. By promoting these lies, under the mantel of revelation, RMN helped create an environment where people would accept the shot, accept public funding for the shot, and even accept mandates for the shot. The humanitarian arm of the church donated 20 million dollars to UNICEF for the COVAX facility from which hundreds of thousands of doses were shipped.[46] In these ways, they were also supporting massive vaccine sales. The fanaticism of the Führer toward a final solution[47] had returned, looking as 'civil' and 'palatable' as Germany's early moves in eradicating what they considered the public health menace of their time (the Jews).[48]

In Australia, police beat down unarmed women for walking down the street without a mask. They set out to build multiple concentration camps, one holding over 2000 unvaxxed persons with punishments for escape.[49] In Austria, CNBC reported that police conducted "'random

---

[46] "Church donations aiding UNICEF's role in the global effort to provide 2 billion COVID-19 vaccinations", Scott Taylor, Church News, 30 April 2021. https://www.thechurchnews.com/2021/4/30/23217280/latter-day-saint-charities-unicef-global-covid-19-vaccinations.

[47] "It is more than just irony that Bill Gates said, "the final solution—which is a year or two years off—is the vaccine." Episode 378 *The Corbett Report*, 8 May 2020, https://www.corbettreport.com/gatesvaccine/

[48] The oppression, dehumanization, and eventual atrocities of Germany against the Jews were also done in the name of public health. "Physicians and medically trained academics, many of whom were proponents of "racial hygiene," or eugenics, legitimized and helped to implement Nazi policies aiming to "cleanse" German society of people viewed as biologic threats to the nation's health." From "In the Name of Public Health—Nazi Racial Hygiene," Susan Bachrach, Ph.D., New England Medical Journal, 29 July 2004, pp. 417-420. https://www.ushmm.org/m/pdfs/07192004-nazi-racial-hygiene-bachrach.pdf, see also "Propaganda Poster: "Jews Are Lice: They Cause Typhus", Public Health Under the Third Reich, U.S. Holocaust Memorial Museum, https://perspectives.ushmm.org/item/propaganda-poster-jews-are-lice-they-cause-typhus/collection/public-health-under-the-third-reich.

[49] "'You feel like you're in prison. You feel like you've done something wrong, it's inhumane what they're doing. You are so small; they just overpower you. And you're literally nothing. It's like 'you do what we say, or you're in trouble, we'll lock you up for longer'. Yeah, they were even threatening me that if I was to do this again, "we will extend your time in here," said detainee, Hayley Hodgson, 26, who never tested positive over her 14-day imprisonment at the camp, "Any rules necessary:" Villa Park Democrat Conroy bill would create Illinois concentration camps for non Covid-vaxxed", Dupage Policy Journal, https://dupagepolicyjournal.com/stories/619606613-any-rules-necessary-villa-park-democrat-conroy-bill-would-create-illinois-concentration-camps-for-non-covid-vaxxed, 2 Feb 2022

checks' to ensure compliance with Covid-19 lockdowns for the country's 2 million unvaccinated residents. There, "the unvaccinated are not allowed in public spaces."[50] In Canada, the police pulled a taser on a lone teenager who remained on an outdoor hockey rink.[51] The Canadian government directed banks to take money directly out of the bank accounts of those protesting vaccine mandates.[52] Canadian police shot an unarmed reporter at point blank range.[53] Even at the time of this writing in October 2022, California passed a law that would take away the license of doctors who deviate from the mandated protocol for Covid treatment.[54]

The Spirit of Persecution Offers Rewards (Spoils)

"But behold, Satan did stir up the hearts of the more part of the Nephites, **insomuch that they did unite with those bands of robbers,**[55] **and did enter into their covenants and their oaths***, that they would protect and preserve one another in whatsoever difficult circumstances they should be placed"* (Helaman 6:21).

On October 14th 2020 Elder Bednar made an address to the G20 Interfaith Forum.[56] Much of what he said was valid recognition that

[50] Ibid.
[51] "PUNISHED for PLAYING HOCKEY: Calgary police threaten to TASER young skater at outdoor rink", Keean Bexte, Rebel News, https://www.rebelnews.com/punished_for_playing_hockey_calgary_police_threaten_to_taser_young_skater_at_outdoor_rink, 20 Dec 2020.
[52] https://thehighwire.com/videos/canada-heats-up-freezes-accounts/
[53] https://thehighwire.com/videos/reporter-shot-by-police-at-point-blank-range/
[54] "California passes law to silence doctors who don't subscribe to COVID 'contemporary scientific consensus'", Sharyl Attkisson, Sharyl Attkisson: Untouchable Subjects. Fearless. Nonpartisan Reporting. 24 Oct 2022. https://sharylattkisson.com/2022/10/california-passes-law-to-silence-doctors-who-dont-subscribe-to-covid-contemporary-scientific-consensus/
[55] Dr. Mark Trozzi, MD in Canada describes how the medical establishment united in criminal behavior: "Bizarrely, in these colleges in Canada [like the licensing College of Physicians and Surgeons], like around the world…everything they are doing is unlawful, they're the criminals clearly … By blocking the treatment of COVID… about 85% of the people that died, died because of them and because of how **they twisted all the doctor's arms into violating the Hippocratic oath and *joining in this criminal scheme***" ("Doctors Speaking Out Against the Narrative are being Suspended and Attacked" 22:45-23:20, CHD Europe, Dr. Mark Trozzi, https://drtrozzi.org/2023/01/11/ca-persecution-of-ethical-drs-draws-international-attention/ , 11 Jan 2023).
[56] His 8 min monologue available online here: https://www.facebook.com/watch/?v=273057890486610

religion should not be regarded as "non-essential," but in his defense of these values, he made an unabashed appeal to form a partnership with government institutions to promote their version of events, endorse their information, and even "debunk" opposing voices by providing "accurate" information. These damning statements show complicity with the forces behind the corruption of the Covid-19 era, reminiscent of uniting with those bands of robbers, entering into "their covenants and their oaths" in a quid pro quo arrangement. "Government and policymakers can win allies," he promised, if they would work with religious leaders.

Do prisoners of war want one of their leaders to promise their captors that they can win allies if they offer better benefits to the agreeable segment of the prisoners in the camp? No.

In his video, he labels those opposing government measures as irresponsible by saying "responsible voices in the faith community" are congruent with government policies and intentions. This was a clear indication that the Church had no interest in representing 'irresponsible voices' who were not in agreement with the vaccine-promoting governments of the world.

He follows up with a clarification of how this suggested alliance would look like:

"Religion can be a powerful source of legitimacy and practical assistance in a time of crisis…. Misinformation is a major obstacle in a health crisis. Faith communities can debunk rumors, calm fears, and facilitate accurate information. Many will be fearful of vaccines; religious leaders can be helpful in the fight against the coronavirus" [in other words getting our parishioners to take the vaccine they are so 'fearful of']."

He then closes this power couple description of worldly government and religious power reiterating the quid pro quo of the arrangement:

"Respecting the dignity of religious people pays important dividends."

By itself, that statement could be defended as describing an important truth, if the dividends are defined as greater love in a community, an increase of the Spirit of God working at all levels of society. At the start of his eight-minute speech, Elder Bednar mentioned the fact that faith communities transmit moral and social truths to the next generation. If he had continued in that vein, and made a case for religious freedom based on those facts, there would be nothing of concern.

But these are not the dividends he focused on while enticing world governments to give his institution a seat at the table. Instead, he tried to show how he can further the corrupt goals of the power drunk gild – squash dissent, promote an oppressive government agenda, and use positions of trust to convince the population to inject biological poison into their bodies.

"Respect people like me, and the masses will eat out of your hand;" these were the flavor of the dividends he was offering.

For those aware, reading between the lines, they heard:

"Having trouble with those unruly and pesky lovers of freedom and truth that keep noticing that the emperor is wearing no clothes? Not to worry, we will help 'debunk' them, brainwash our people with your self-styled "accurate information" from our position of trust, and in so doing, we will see that those dangerous (to your power) advocates of truth are ignored, ostracized, marginalized, and if we are most successful, made fun of. Is your tyranny not going as smoothly as you like? Well, just let my institution through the doors and we can help put people to sleep, 'calm fears' that their freedom is being taken away, or that your product is the opposite of what you claim it to be, and your tyranny will proceed like a well-oiled machine. You see, a partnership with us pays dividends. So why don't you recognize us, and make an agreement, covenant, and oath, with us; let's be *united* as allies, and it will work out better for both of us. We protect and preserve your lies; you protect and preserve our position. There is no reason we both cannot share in the spoils of crisis, and if you let us in, we'll make sure you increase yours."

Elder Bednar is a powerful speaker. I have used his "parable of the pickle" many times to illustrate the importance of consistent exertion in living the gospel, like daily scripture study. It is sad to see his talents used to promise the influence of church leaders as a tool to further corrupt government propaganda. Three months after Bednar's address, the First Presidency made public their support of all the sales points of the government leaders and pharmaceutical companies trying to sell the jab.

The First Presidency messages issued worldwide to the church were not issued as individuals hoping to persuade others on what they thought was the best course from their point of view or based on their scientific or medical backgrounds, but as ecclesiastical leaders who had superior knowledge. Many members of the church saw the First Presidency letters as "the word of the Lord," thinking they must apply the following scripture no matter how incongruent to RMN; "whether by my mouth or the voice of my servants it is the same."[57] They incorrectly interpreted this scripture to mean anything RMN said was the word of the Lord. Within most influential circles of the church, to question whether the vaccine was a "literal godsend," as RMN said it was, or whether the vaccine was actually safe and effective, was no less than questioning God himself.

For many truth seekers in the church, the 12 August 2021 letter from the First Presidency increased the levels of persecution and

---

[57] Doctrine and Covenants 1:37-38. A very good discussion of this scripture and related principles is in Section 4 of this article: "Fact-Checking Misquoted Statement on Blindly Following the Prophet", James F. Stoddard III and L. Hannah Stoddard, Joseph Smith Foundation, https://josephsmithfoundation.org/fact-checking-misquoted-statements-on-blindly-following-the-prophet/?fbclid=IwAR2agST40gexkXD3WljKIbrNO-6rN_6f0UT06K0BZESruo5UlrVWKj3pU4c.

derision they felt, amplifying the derision from the public space into one's closest friends and associates in their own faith, and even their own homes. One stake president said of this period how interesting it was that this period became a "litmus test." He was evidently referring to how closely someone would unquestioningly follow a lie as proper loyalty to a prophet. A religion professor at Utah State University voiced the same sentiment: "The common perception of Mormons and Mormonism is that when church leaders speak, church members listen and do what they're told," said Mason. "This has revealed sometimes how conditional that loyalty can be."[58] They were both right in a way they did not intend; it *was* a litmus test, and revealing of loyalty—of those who cared more to search for and be loyal to **truth**, versus those who preferred comfort and social acceptance. Those who diligently sought knowledge of the truth themselves versus those who preferred to rely on the word of a man in the false security that loyalty to man is all that is needed for salvation. The lazy way appeals to the majority,[59] and this period formed into lockstep, even mass psychosis,[60] those people enticed by it.

Jeremiah 23 is a powerful chapter not only because of its prophecies of the last days, (as he says "in the latter days ye shall consider it [i.e. understand it] perfectly"), but also in how it reveals the Lord's thoughts upon recognizing lies coming from prophets:

---

[58] https://news.yahoo.com/mormon-vaccine-push-ratchets-dividing-041316188.html
[59] "That's scary because, yes, but there is always 60 or 65% of the people who do not really go along with the narrative but who will never speak out, who will always choose the easy way and go along with the people—with this group of people [30%] that seems to have the loudest voice. That's why, in the end, up to 95% or, sometimes even more, go along with the totalitarian narrative—with the narrative that led to the mass formation. And there is an additional 5% that doesn't go along with it, that tries to speak out. And that's extremely important if you understand the mechanism of mass formation, if you really understand it, then you know what this small group should do" (Mattias Desmet, Tucker Carlson Tonight, https://www.foxnews.com/video/6311668288112, 31 Aug 2022. .
[60] "Totalitarian mass psychosis does not just arise organically, however. Rather it is deliberately inculcated by the ruling class." Hughes, Kyrie & Broudy, *Unlimited Hangout*, "Covid -19 Mass Formation or Mass Atrocity" 29 Nov 2022. https://unlimitedhangout.com/2022/11/investigative-reports/covid-19-mass-formation-or-mass-atrocity/

Jeremiah 23: 1-2: Woe be unto the pastors that destroy and scatter the sheep of my pasture saith the Lord! Therefore, thus saith the Lord God of Israel against the pastors that feed my people; Ye have scattered my flock and driven them away, **and have not been *mindful* of them**, behold I will visit upon you the evil of your doings, saith the Lord.

The actions of RMN were not mindful of those who wanted to avoid the wicked promotions of the vaccine and supporting the cabal behind it.

Jeremiah 23:11: "For both the prophet and priest are profane; yea, in my house have I found their wickedness, saith the Lord."

In verse 11, we find profaneness could have been translated as irreligious (footnote c in the LDS printing of the Bible). RMN's emphasis on trusting in the lies of man is irreligious.

Jeremiah 23:14: I have seen also in the prophets of Jerusalem a horrible thing: they commit adultery, and walk in lies: **they strengthen also the hands of evildoers**, that none doth return from his wickedness: they are all of them unto me as Sodom, and the inhabitants thereof as Gomorrah. **:15**…for from the prophets of Jerusalem is profaneness gone forth into all the land. [Like a world-wide letter].

Jeremiah 23:16: Thus saith the Lord of hosts, hearken not unto the words of the prophets that prophesy unto you: they make you **vain**: they speak a vision of their own heart, and not out of the mouth of the Lord.

The words of RMN made people vain. Taking vain action and hope in taking a harmful shot, thinking that by so doing they stopped transmission of Covid-19 with the possibility of eradicating it, thinking they were protecting themselves and others from Covid-19 when none of that was true.

Though not new to any following the facts, European parliament members were shocked when a vice president from Pfizer told them the shot was never tested to see if it stopped transmission.[61] "We want to do all we can to limit the spread of these viruses," RMN said as he prefaced his urging to take the shot. The shot became a symbol of humility, righteousness, and piety, and in vain demonstrations many members of the church took the shot (who otherwise would have avoided it) as a symbol of their faith in the prophet and loyalty to him, "to limit the spread."

In summary, these were our days: a prophet teaching lies, a U.S. president at the head persecuting any who could see past the lies, church government offering their church members as a sacrifice to powers of government, and church members led to err in vain ambitions which enriched their captors, all buoyed on a bed of false promises. We saw corporations, leaders, elites, and government institutions hiding the results of vaccine trials and lying about vaccine efficacy and safety, with the end result of increasing infection, death, and injury,[62] all for an increase in power and gain for those who promoted the lie.

Can we not hear the echoes of Moroni's warning in Ether chapter 8?

23 Wherefore, O ye Gentiles, it is wisdom in God that these things should be shown unto you, that thereby ye may repent of your sins, **and suffer not that these murderous combinations shall get above**

---

[61] Robert Roos, European Parliament member from the Netherlands, received a direct answer from Pfizer that the vaccine's ability to prevent transmission was never tested. See the clip of when it happened, along with his commentary with Tucker Carlson on Robert Roos's Twitter page here: https://twitter.com/Rob_Roos/status/1580194898791354371?s=20&t=CXPLvKrt79kyFnJLE_5D5Q. Also see it here: https://www.fox2detroit.com/video/1129402; and here https://twitter.com/Rob_Roos/status/1579759795225198593?s=20&t=25QVicCAoX0tYDhl8lhn9g

[62] "According to a recent study, mRNA COVID-19 vaccines were associated with an excess risk of serious adverse events, including coagulation disorders, acute cardiac injuries, Bell's palsy, and encephalitis, to name a few. This risk was 1 in 550, much higher than other vaccines. To claim these vaccines are "safe and effective" while minimizing and disregarding the adverse events is unconscionable." From a letter to the FDA by Joseph A. Ladapo, MD, PhD, Florida Surgeon General. Episode 324. https://thehighwire.com/ark-videos/when-two-universes-collide/

you, which are built up to get ª<u>power</u> and gain—and the work, yea, even the work of ᵇ<u>destruction</u> come upon you, yea, even the sword of the justice of the Eternal God shall fall upon you, to your overthrow and destruction if ye shall suffer these things to be.

24 Wherefore, **the Lord commandeth you, when ye shall see these things come among you that ye shall awake to a sense of your awful situation,** because of this ª<u>secret combination</u> which shall be among you; or **wo be unto it, because of the blood of them who have been slain;** for they cry from the dust for vengeance upon it, and also upon those who built it up.

25 For it cometh to pass that whoso buildeth it up seeketh to overthrow the ª<u>freedom</u> of all lands, nations, and countries; and it bringeth to pass the destruction of all people, for it is built up by the devil, **who is the father of all lies;** even that same liar who ᵇ<u>beguiled</u> our first parents, yea, even that same liar who hath caused man to commit murder from the beginning; who hath ᶜ<u>hardened</u> the hearts of men that they have ᵈ<u>murdered</u> the prophets, and stoned them, and cast them out from the beginning.

What did Moroni mean by "murderous combination"?

In the 1828 dictionary we find combination means "intimate union, or association of two or more persons or things, by set purpose or agreement, for effecting some object, by joint operation . . . It is sometimes equivalent to league, or to conspiracy."[63]

As a member of the Catholic Church, and his own Pope taking the same positions as RMN, Archbishop Vigano felt the spirit of awakening to our awful situation. In an open letter to other archbishops, he wrote:

"This means therefore that there is a grave moral obligation to refuse inoculation as a possible and proximate cause of permanent damages or death. In the absence of benefits, there is therefore no

---
[63] *American Dictionary of the English Language*, "Combination," https://webstersdictionary1828.com/Dictionary/evil.

need to expose oneself to the risks of its administration, but on the contrary, there is a duty to refuse it categorically."

"The silence of so many Cardinals and Bishops, along with the inconceivable promotion of the vaccination campaign by the Holy See, represents a form of unprecedented complicity that cannot continue any longer. **It is necessary to denounce this scandal, this crime against humanity, this satanic action against God.**"

"I realize that it may be extremely unpopular to take a position against the so-called vaccines, but as Shepherds of the flock of the Lord **we have the duty to denounce the horrible crime that is being carried out, whose goal is to create billions of chronically ill people and to exterminate millions and millions of people**, based on the infernal ideology of the "Great Reset" formulated by the President of the World Economic Forum Klaus Schwab and endorsed by institutions and organizations around the world." (Emphasis added, Letter #136, 2021, Wed, Oct 27: Archbishop Viganò's Open Letter to Archbishop Gomez).[64]

Archbishop Vigano awakened. Should *we* not *also* awaken?

---

[64]Vigano continued: "With every passing day, thousands of people are dying or are being affected in their health by the illusion that the so-called vaccines guarantee a solution to the pandemic emergency. The Catholic Church has the duty before God and all of humanity to denounce this tremendous and horrible crime with the utmost firmness, giving clear directions and taking a stand against those who, in the name of a pseudo-science subservient to the interests of the pharmaceutical companies and the globalist elite, **have only intentions of death**." See the full text here along with references to Vigano's sources in his letter: "Letter #136, 2021, Wed, Oct 27: Viganò to Gomez", Inside The Vatican, https://insidethevatican.com/news/newsflash/letter-136-2021-wed-oct-27-vigano-to-gomez/.

Chapter 3: Intellectual Gymnastics

While the lies being taught by RMN were recognized by many, the intellectual gymnastics to attempt to square these lies and still recognize him as a true and living prophet were many and varied.

It is true, RMN is called of God and appointed the prophet and president of the church. It is only as a prophet that the scriptures mentioned in this book are relevant. It was prophesied, by Isaiah, Ezekial, Jeremiah, and by quotation, Nephi, that prophets would teach lies. Sometimes that happens. Even prophets have agency. Even prophets can be deceived. Instead of coming up with fairy tales and intricate theories to explain RMN's un-prophetic behavior, we should instead look to see how God handles these kinds of situations. He explains it, in Isaiah, and Jeremiah, and Ezekial in particular. The Book of Mormon is not suddenly untrue because RMN supports the money-making schemes of a drug maker. His actions do not change the truthfulness of what the Lord has restored and revealed any more than Jonah refusing to preach repentance (for a time) could change the need of Assyria to repent. However, the fact that God takes care of it (he realigns the direction in his own time) does not change the lies taught from being lies, or from being harmful.

What do the faithful do in such times? They look to the Lord. They heed the lesson of the younger prophet in 1 Kings 13.

In this chapter we see the man of God performing a mission of returning home after calling Israel to repentance for their idolatry. He prophesies of a future king. He prophesies their alter will be rent, after which the king commands to capture the young prophet and as he does so his arm dries up so he cannot pull it back. He begs the man of God for help. The young prophet heals him, and the alter is rent. The king, so grateful and impressed, invites the young prophet to dine with him. In this case the young prophet states "I will not go in with thee, neither will I eat bread nor drink water in this place: for so was it charged me by the word of the Lord saying, Eat no bread, nor drink water, nor turn again by the same way that thou camest" (v. 9-10). The man of God succeeds in diffusing the temptation of government power and its enticements but chooses instead the path Lord chose for him.

Then comes the old prophet who tells him, "Come home with me, and eat bread." At first the young prophet refuses, rightly so, because the Lord had given him specific instructions *not* to do just that kind of activity. But the senior prophet insists, "I am a prophet also as thou art and an angel spake unto me by the word of the Lord, saying, Bring him back with them into the house, that he may eat bread and drink water." The young prophet concedes and goes with the older prophet.

While the King James translation says the senior prophet lied about the angel, we learn through Joseph Smith that the Lord told the senior prophet to say what he said, "That I may prove him; and he lied *not* unto him" **(JST 1 King 13:18)**.

An angel really did appear to the senior prophet, and tell the senior prophet to make an invitation contrary to the mission that the Lord expected the younger prophet to follow. The man of God passed the test of government enticing against the will of the Lord, could he also pass the test of the enticing of a prophet against the will of the Lord? I.E., could the man of God be more faithful and loyal to the Lord than to a prophet?[65]

---

[65]It may seem odd that God would test loyalty to Him over other goodness, like following a prophet, but it is not odd. The appetites of the flesh tempt men and women to break the law of chastity by having sexual relations outside of marriage. Some have genuine love and admiration for the person with whom they would compromise God's law. Even if combined with physical appetite and lust, many times, it is sincere love that initially brings them together. Yet even something as good as genuine love cannot be an excuse for disobeying God. God

The answer in this case was that he failed. Instead of trusting the Lord, he trusted the prophet. His recompense: "Forasmuch as thou hast disobeyed the mouth of the Lord…thy carcass shall not come unto the sepulcher of thy fathers" (**v. 21-22**). Before he made it home, he was killed by a lion.

This exact situation had never happened previously; the young prophet had nothing to compare his experience to exactly. It is quite unlikely that we will ever again have this exact situation repeat itself; a king reprimanded in the middle of idol worship, a prophet cursing the king's arm so the king can't bring it back, then heal it again and have the king thank him. However, what we see in this story is the character of God, *His* priorities, *His* expectations. These are bedrock truths that the sensitive seeker of truth can apply to innumerable situations (and underscores why it is so important to study the scriptures—to come to know the character of God Himself).

This is an amazing doctrine for some, and many have been raised to believe that the word of the prophet is mandatorily synonymous with the word of the Lord. Such a belief can lead to laziness as a people spiritually atrophy in seeking their own witness of the will of the Lord.[66] What this scriptural account shows us, is that the Lord must come first in our lives, even ahead of a beloved prophet. If the path the Lord has told us to take is different from the path the prophet has told us to take, then we listen to the Lord over the prophet and follow the Lord's direction. As wisely stated at the Joseph Smith Foundation: "Some of our leaders are placed there to lead us, and others of our leaders are placed there to test us."[67]

---

has commanded that sexual relations not occur outside of marriage. God requires obedience and loyalty to Him over any expression of love or loyalty for another.

[66]"Now those men, or those women, who know no more about the Holy Spirit, than to be led entirely by another person, suspending their own understanding, and pinning their faith upon another's sleeve, will never be capable of entering into the celestial glory," Brigham Young. JD 1:312, https://scriptures.byu.edu/#:t273c:j01 .

[67]This entire article is well worth a thoughtful study: "10 Largely Forgotten, but Timeless Principles, in Sustaining Leaders", James F. Stoddard III and L. Hannah Stoddard, Joseph Smith Foundation, https://josephsmithfoundation.org/10-largely-forgotten-but-timeless-principles-in-sustaining-leaders/.

President Oaks told the young adults during one fireside:

"As a General Authority, I have the responsibility to preach general principles. When I do, I don't try to define all the exceptions. There are exceptions to some rules ... don't ask me to give an opinion on your exception. I only teach the general rules. Whether an exception applies to you is your responsibility. You must work that out individually between you and the Lord" ("Dating versus Hanging Out", Church Educational System Fireside, 1 May 2005).

Through the Covid-19 plandemic, one criticism voiced against those who chose to not get the vaccine was, "how could God provide you revelation different from the prophet?" A similar concern was vocalized by a member of the Church to an AP reporter, referring to members who would not take the shot she said, "why would you choose the side that doesn't include your faith leader?"[68] The record of 1 Kings 13 shows in principle and specifics not only why this *can* be the case, but that such situations are also a tool the Lord specifically uses in proving his servants faithful to His word and loyal to Him above all else.

Nevertheless, not understanding this doctrine, many came up with excuse after excuse, or intellectual gymnastics, for the prophet teaching lies. Various rationale surfaced, here are a few:

- Some said, "*It's actually a great master plan, he is supposed to say pro-vaccine rhetoric to keep 501(c)3 (tax-exempt) status for the Church, but he doesn't really want us to get vaccinated.*"

- False – he really did want church members to get it, and even if he did not, many did get it because of his statements.

- Some said, "*He is a president of a corporation, as well as president of the Church, he is only saying to get the vaccine as a president of a corporation, not as the prophet.*"

---

[68] https://news.yahoo.com/mormon-vaccine-push-ratchets-dividing-041316188.html

False – He wrote the letters under the letterhead and signature of the First Presidency of the church, not as president of a corporation.

- Some say, "*He is supposed to bring the Church out of order so that it can be put back in order before the second coming.*"

To this the Lord's words seem an appropriate reply, "it must needs be that offences come; but woe to that man by whom the offence cometh!"[69]

- Some took this position: "*We have to do everything in our power to keep the temples open – even if it means telling the lies of the establishment (even if those lies result in the deaths of innocents and the robbery of a nation).*"

The Lord had an answer for such attitudes in Jeremiah's day:

"Trust ye not in lying words, saying, The temple of the Lord, The temple of the Lord, The temple of the Lord, are these ... Therefore, will I do unto this house, which is called by my name, wherein ye trust, and unto the place which I gave to you and to your fathers, as I have done to Shiloh [which was destroyed] ... For the children of Judah have done evil in my sight, saith the Lord; they have set their abominations in the house which is called by my name, to pollute it" (Jeremiah 7: 4,14,30).

The Old Testament Institute manual explains well what is happening here:

"The boldness of Jeremiah's statement can be realized only when one recalls the importance given to the temple by the reforms of Josiah in 621 B.C. Josiah had made it the sole place of sacrificial worship of Jehovah for all Jews in an attempt to stamp out idol worship. **The**

---

[69]Matt 18:7. Many erudite pontificators like to imagine Judas betraying Jesus as some part of a righteous scheme as well. Jesus quells this position as recorded in Luke 22:22 "And truly the Son of man goeth, as it was determined: but woe unto that man by whom he is betrayed!"

temple and its priests thus had acquired by this time greater importance than ever before ... He [Jeremiah] plainly told the Jews that if they would mend their ways and become righteous, they would be spared; **otherwise, not even the temple would save them, because they had made the temple a "*den of robbers*"** (v. 11). Because of the great reverence the people had for the temple, **though it was a false reverence**, it is not surprising that Jeremiah was quickly arrested and imprisoned (Jeremiah 26) .... **For the wicked to look to the temple as a source of protection was foolish.** Jeremiah (7:21-23) reminded the people that obedience [to God] is more critical to God than the outward rituals of sacrifice performed in the temple" (Old Testament Religion 302 Student Manual 1 Kings- Malachi, 2nd ed, p. 238, The Church of Jesus Christ of Latter-day Saints, 1982, emphasis added)[70]

To use the temple as an excuse to promote wickedness is no excuse at all in the eyes of the Lord.

- Some said, *"We can't say or notice that President Nelson is teaching lies because that would be evil speaking of the Lord's anointed."*

Is it evil to call evil what it is?[71] And who is the Lord's anointed? *The*

---

[70]Keil and Delitzsch also have commentary making the same point with respect to Jer 7:14: "The temple is to undergo the fate of the former sanctuary at Shiloh. This threat is introduced by a grounding כִּי, for. This 'for' refers to **the central idea of the last verse, that they must not build their expectations on the temple, hold it to be a pledge for their safety.** For since the Lord has seen how they have profaned and still profane it, He will destroy it, as the sanctuary at Shiloh was destroyed ... They were to behold with their own eyes the fate of the sanctuary at Shiloh, that **so they might understand that the sacredness of a place does not save it from overthrow, if men have desecrated it by their wickedness**" (Keil and Delitzsch Biblical Commentary on the Old Testament, biblehub.com). Also, Matthew Henry's commentary, "No observances, professions, or supposed revelations, will profit, if men do not amend their ways and their doings. None can claim an interest in free salvation, who allow themselves in the practice of known sin, **or live in the neglect of known duty. They thought that the temple they profaned would be their protection**" (Matthew Henry's Concise Commentary, Biblehub.com), https://biblehub.com/commentaries/jeremiah/7-14.htm.

[71]Machiavelli, the notorious observer of political power, noted of church leaders in his day, **"they got them to believe that it is evil to speak ill even of what is evil**; and that it is good to be obedient to rulers, who, if they do amiss, may be left to the judgment of God. By which teaching, these rulers are encouraged to behave as badly as they can, having no fear of

Anointed is Christ. In fact, the word "Christ" comes from the Greek "Christos" which means "the anointed one."[72] Jesus is the Christ, the anointed one. To attribute lies to Him would actually be speaking evil of him. To endorse lies as truth because the lies are spoken by one of His servants is to speak evil of the Anointed. If we cannot admit error for a church leader, would we then condone and participate in the embezzlement of tithing funds because it was directed by a bishop or stake president? Can we plan the massacre of innocents and kill women and children and not be accountable for it because a Stake President orchestrated it (ala the Mountain Medows Massacre)?[73] If we cannot admit error in leadership, how could we ever vote "opposed" to any proposals made in General Conference? If we can never vote "opposed" then why is the question asked, "any opposed?"

From the 1828 Webster's dictionary (a very useful dictionary for understanding language at it was understood at the founding of the church) 'evil' is defined as

1. Having bad qualities of a natural kind; mischievous; having qualities which tend to injury, or to produce mischief.

2. "Having bad qualities of a moral kind; wicked; corrupt; perverse; wrong; as *evil* thoughts; *evil* deeds; *evil* speaking; and *evil* generation.[74]

Observing when leaders have gone astray when measured against the Bible, the Book of Mormon, or the Doctrine and Covenants is speaking in defense of truth, and against its adulteration; otherwise,

---

punishments which they neither see nor credit" (emphasis added). *Discourses on Livy by Niccolo Machiavelli*, p. 174. The Federalist Papers Project, https://thefederalistpapers.org/wp-content/uploads/2013/08/Discourses-on-Livy.pdf.

[72]"Christ the Anointed One", Fr Kenneth Baker, S.J., CERC, https://www.catholiceducation.org/en/culture/catholic-contributions/christ-the-anointed-one.html#:~:text=The%20word%20%22Christ%22%20is%20the%20English%20transliteration%20of,advertisements%20for%20performances%20or%20records%20of%20Handel%27s%20Messiah. 1995.

[73]https://www.churchofjesuschrist.org/study/history/topics/mountain-meadows-massacre?lang=eng

[74]*American Dictionary of the English Language*, "Evil", https://webstersdictionary1828.com/Dictionary/evil.

Isaiah, Ezekiel, and Jeremiah, Abinadi and other prophets would all be condemned for calling other prophets, liars, sinners, adulterers, etc. An example of speaking evil is making plans to murder someone. Speaking evil would be directing and endorsing arrangements to imprison the innocent, or rob their bank accounts and means of employment. Speaking evil includes language which endorses evil deeds and acts such as sodomy, abortion, bestiality, and transgender mutilations. Speaking evil would direct the silencing of words and thoughts that defend truth. Speaking evil would be conspiring to murder a prophet while he lay in his hospital bed.

In a discourse in 1839 Joseph Smith said (as recorded by Willard Richards):

O ye Twelve and all saints profit by this important key [image of a key] that in all your trials, troubles, temptations, afflictions, bonds, imprisonments, and death, see to it that you do not betray heaven, that you do not betray Jesus Christ, that you do not betray your brethren, that you do not betray the revelations of God, neither in the Bible, Book of Mormon or Doctrine & Covenants or any other that ever was or ever will be given and revealed unto men in this world, or in the world to come, yea in all your kickings and flounderings see to it that you do not this thing, **lest innocent blood be found in your skirts**, and you go down to hell. All other sins are not to be compared to sins against the Holy Ghost and proving a traitor to thy brethren. ("Discourse, 2 July 1839, as Reported by William Clayton," p. 1, The Joseph Smith Papers, accessed January 13, 2023, https://www.josephsmithpapers.org/paper-summary/discourse-2-july-1839-as-reported-by-william-clayton/1, emphasis added).

What does it mean to betray heaven? What does it mean to betray Christ? The betrayal Joseph is talking about refers to the shedding of innocent blood and as sinning against the Holy Ghost. Joseph Smith gave us the grand key to recognize speaking evil of church leaders— the desiring of their murder, or the murder of other innocents. We see an example of this evil speaking in 1 Ne 1:13, "And they [Laman and Lemuel] ... sought to take away the life of my father." Those who conspired to kill the prophet Daniel through the machinations of the law is another example of such evil speaking: "Then said these men, We shall not find any occasion against this Daniel, except we find it against him concerning the law of his God" (Dan 6:5), and hence they hatched the plan to feed Daniel to the lions. When Colonel Hinckle secretly agreed to betray Joseph Smith and other church leaders and turn them over to the murderous General Lucas, that was evil speaking and betrayal of the nature Joseph referred.

Christ is the real head of this church. Loyalty and consideration to Him takes precedence over all other loyalties and considerations. When leaders act in opposition to the purposes of Christ, it behooves us to first ensure we are not also acting in opposition to Christ by following the instructions of that leader.

"When we undertake to cover our sins, or to gratify our pride, our vain ambition [such as position in the church], or to exercise control or dominion or compulsion upon the souls of the children of men, in any degree of unrighteousness, behold, the heavens withdraw themselves; the Spirit of the Lord is grieved; and when it is withdrawn, Amen [or sayonara] to the priesthood or the authority of that man" (D&C 121:37).

Intellectual gymnastic feats to keep RMN on a pedestal of infallibility are not necessary. Nor need anyone panic when they discover he has been teaching lies. Joseph Smith said, "The priesthood shall prevail over its enemies, triumph over the devil and be established upon the earth never more to be thrown down."[75] The most important thing is to look to the Lord. What is the path he has commanded? Are you commanded to get the shot? Then get it. Are you commanded not to? Then don't. Neither side should condemn the other for making the choice they believe is God's will for them. Neither do any have need to masquerade that a blatant lie is not a lie. Rather, truth, is the watchword of the faithful.

When Watchmen Help the Enemy

The prophets are the watchmen of our day. The Lord teaches us some principles regarding our responsibility to the watchmen:

"But if the watchman see the sword come, and blow not the trumpet, and the people be not warned; if the sword come, and take any person from among them, he is taken away in his iniquity; but his blood will I require at the watchman's hand" (Ezekiel 33: 2-6)

Who have we set up as our watchman? We have set up Russell M. Nelson as our watchman.

"No, we haven't!", the chorus protests, "he was called by line of succession. He was called of God. The apostles ordained him and we sustained him in General Conference and now he is the prophet." Yes, indeed, but in general conference we voted for him. Our vote was our *personal* responsibility.

Chorus: We voted for him?

Perceptive: Yes.

Chorus: How? When?

Perceptive: When it was proposed that he be sustained as the President of the church, and as prophet, seer, and revelator. When you voted in favor of that proposition, you voted for him, of your own free will. You said, in effect, 'that sounds good to me!' along with everyone else voting for him. 'I want him as my watchman!'

Chorus: So *we* set him up as our watchman?

Perceptive: Yes. You personally did so, with your personal vote.

Chorus: What if he's not doing a very good job as watchman? In fact, what if he has actually helped the enemy through the gates instead of warning us of the enemy? Instead of warning us of the machinations of men to kill, maim, injure, and enslave us in the interest of increasing their own wealth and power. He told us to do exactly what the enemy wanted. That doesn't sound like a watchman to us!

Perceptive: Then what does it sound like?

Chorus: An accomplice.

Perceptive: So what will do you do now?

Chorus: Well, we don't want him as our watchman.

Perceptive: So what will you do now?

Chorus: --

Perceptive: Why do you keep voting in favor of something that you oppose? When it is again proposed that he remain as our watchman, as president of the church, will you vote for him again?

(Simultaneously) Chorus A: No. Chorus B: Yes Chorus C: --

Perceptive: When you stand before God to be judged of your works, do you want to be responsible for his actions? For the blood of those who die because they took the vaccines? For the works that were promoted by his support of the liars who sought to enrich and take power to themselves via a systematic attack on the population? No? Then why would you vote for him?

Chorus B: We're embarrassed. What will people say of us?

Chorus C: And besides wouldn't we lose our temple recommends if we don't vote for him?

Perceptive (to Chorus B): To those who are embarrassed, who do you fear more, God or man?

Perceptive (to Chorus C): Why should you lose your temple recommend? You are being asked a question on a proposal, on an option. If you are only allowed to answer one way, it would not be a vote would it? It would be a test. In this case, it is a vote on a proposal. Similar to a vote in the "committee of the whole" during the constitutional convention of the United States. If you vote against, you will be asked to talk with your stake president, and you can tell him why you voted against. This is different from the temple recommend question when you affirm that the President of the Church is the president of the church. It is like when a military member goes to the ballot box. He can vote against the sitting president, but still be loyal to the constitutional government where that president sits as an incumbent. Similarly, a member of the church can vote against a proposed make-up of the First Presidency but still sustain the leaders in promoting the work of the Lord when the membership of the church as a whole has confirmed these to be their leaders.

There have been many asking questions and having conversations similar to these. One writer commented:

"Sometimes we as members forget that the Church of Jesus Christ of Latter-day Saints is just as much our church as it is the church of any leader. Stated another way, we are just as valuable in and accountable for the Church's progress as the current sitting president is. We may not hold keys to alter or make great changes where they may be needed but we can fulfill our sacred roles in defending the Gospel of Jesus Christ."[76]

I heard of a general authority who remarked that the general authorities have not seen the attitude of the members of the church "this bad since Kirtland." This comment is grossly accusatory and erroneous. Those who recognize the lies taught by RMN are not threatening him with his life. On the contrary, many of us still sustain

---

[76] "10 Largely Forgotten, but Timeless Principles, in Sustaining Leaders", James F. Stoddard III and L. Hannah Stoddard, Joseph Smith Foundation, section 4, https://josephsmithfoundation.org/10-largely-forgotten-but-timeless-principles-in-sustaining-leaders/, accessed 27 Jan 2023.

him as the president of the church, called of God and appointed to be the prophet, seer, and revelator, for the world. Though we may still vote against his continued occupancy of that role when given the opportunity in General and Ward Conference. But there is another major difference here. The problems that precipitated many of the problems in Kirtland were because people did not follow the counsel of the prophet, which led to financial ruin for many of them.[77] In the modern case, those that followed the counsel of RMN are the ones encountering ruin as consequences of the vaccine curse their lives: blood clots, strokes, autoimmune dysfunctions, heart problems, cancer (rate triples with vaccination), violent recurrence cancer in what has been termed "turbo cancer", miscarriages, infertility (Australia, one of the top vaccinated countries had 70% decrease in birth rate), and like the man of God in 1 Kings 13, death.[78]

Robert Malone, the original inventor of mRNA technology, remarked, "there seems to be a movement in modern society to avoid information, theories, or opinions that trigger cognitive dissonance and associated psychological pain." He set out in his book *Lies My Gov't Told Me* to provide "a recitation of the lies and harms that have been inflicted on all of us."[79] To attempt to cancel and silence the truth about the lies promoted from RMN's pulpit, authorities have invoked the persecution of the past to paint with the same color any who recognize the lies which RMN taught, and the harms that have come from those lies. Kirtland's experience from our experience now is totally different, and to use such slander against the honest in heart, *who seek no ill against anyone*, is itself persecution.

[77] Joseph Smith said, "The enemy abroad, and apostates in our midst, united their schemes . . . and became disaffected toward me as though I were the sole cause of those very evils I was most strenuously striving against, which were actually brought upon us by the brethren not giving heed to my counsel". 1 June 1837. "History, 1838–1856, volume B-1 [1 September 1834–2 November 1838]," p. 761, The Joseph Smith Papers, https://www.josephsmithpapers.org/paper-summary/history-1838-1856-volume-b-1-1-september-1834-2-november-1838/215

[78] https://thenewamerican.com/covid-vaccine-evil-corrupt-heinous-vile-villainous-wicked-poison-injurious-and-satanic/ (Ben Armstrong show Dec 26th, 2022). Died Suddenly Documentary https://www.independentsentinel.com/died-suddenly-documentary-fact-checked-without-bias/.

[79] *Lies My Gov't Told Me: And the Better Future Coming*, Robert M. Malone, p. 35. Skyhorse Publishing 2022. Kindle.

However, the observant recognizes that RMN is called of God **and appointed**. It is in being so appointed that he fulfills Isaiah's prophecy as the prophet who teacheth lies. Not a false prophet who teacheth lies, but *called of God and appointed*. If it were not so, his lies would not fulfill prophecy. Fauci has been lying since the 1980's (see *The Real Anthony Fauci* by RFK Jr), but his lies do not fulfill the prophecy as he was not called as a prophet of God. Not until RMN started teaching Fauci's lies, with Biden at the head, testifying that the Covid-19 vaccine was safe and effective, and that the *only* way to come out of the pandemic was for a large uptake of the vaccine, only then were these lies from a person who could fulfill the prophecy of a prophet teaching lies.

What is to become of those who follow these teachings? What is the result of holding to a lie? Isaiah declares, ***"For the leaders of this people cause them to err; and they that are led of them are destroyed."***

Who is being destroyed? All ages groups saw a dramatic increase of all-cause mortality (see appendix 3). After the vaccine, the working age population saw a 40% increase in all-cause mortality. Miscarriages skyrocketed across all highly vaccinated populations and nations of the world.[80]

The Lord warned his people. From D&C 112:

24 Behold, vengeance cometh speedily upon the inhabitants of the earth, a day of wrath, a day of burning, a day of desolation, of weeping, of mourning, and of lamentation; and as a whirlwind it shall come upon all the face of the earth, saith the Lord.

25 And upon my house shall it begin and from my house shall it go forth, saith the Lord;

26 First among those among you, saith the Lord, who have professed to know my name and have not known me, and have blasphemed against me in the midst of my house, saith the Lord.

---

[80] Watch the *Died Suddenly* documentary. https://www.bitchute.com/video/PrivMeVOcCed/.

It is essential to recognize that when the Lord says "my house," he sometimes refers to the United States of America, the cradle of freedom where the restoration of the gospel could occur.

With all that is now known on the lies promoted to make and take the vaccine to market, of the harm it has caused, and its complete lack of efficacy, intellectual denial of these facts is becoming much more difficult, and more obvious when the ignorance is purposeful. Indeed, "ignorance" comes from the action word "ignore". At this point, with so much fraud in plain sight, ignorance becomes more and more a choice to ignore. Whether church leaders or even the president of the church choose to remain ignorant or not, our calling is to stand in defense of truth and the Gospel of Jesus Christ. Instead of spending our strength in contortions of excuse for the actions of others, it is much simpler to focus our strength as Joseph Smith said we should:

"It is our duty to concentrate all our influence to make popular that which is sound and good, and unpopular that which is unsound. Tis right politically for a man who has influence to use it, as well as for a man who has no influence to use his: from henceforth I will maintain all the influence I can get. In relation to politics I will speak as a man; but in relation to religion I will speak in authority." (emphasis added)[81]

---

[81]"History Draft [1 January–3 March 1843]," p. 22, The Joseph Smith Papers, accessed March 22, 2023, https://www.josephsmithpapers.org/paper-summary/history-draft-1-january-3-march-1843/24

Chapter 4: Literal Godsend

And upon my house shall it begin and from my house shall it go forth, saith the Lord; first among those among you, saith the Lord, who have professed to know my name and have not known me, and have blasphemed against me in the midst of my house, saith the Lord. (D&C 112:25,26)

What does it look like to profess to know the name of the Lord and yet not know the Lord? The pharisees gave an example of this. Even with the Savior walking among them, they did not recognize their Lord, despite professing great works and loyalty in and to his name. Who did recognize him? We have an example in Peter[82]:

Jesus: Whom say ye that I am?

Peter: Thou art the Christ, the Son of the living God.

Jesus: Blessed art thou, Simon Bar-Jona: for flesh and blood have not revealed it unto thee, but my Father which is in heaven.

Peter did not know Christ because the president of the Sanhedrin or the Rabbi of his childhood told him to believe Jesus. He knew Christ because he trusted the witness of the Father.

The Lord prophesies that in our day there would be those who professed to know His name, but would not know Him. The fact that they profess to know shows us they are public about their devotion. They will *appear* religious. They may even show marked outward signs of publicly accepted illustrations of piety, like taking a vaccine, but they will not know *Him*. They will not know what Jesus really thinks on the matter. In either their naiveté or their ignorance, they will act in ways contrary the Lord's desires.

[82]Matt 16:15-17

The Lord further adds the descriptor—those who blaspheme in his Holy House.

Noah Webster's 1828 dictionary records this definition for "Blaspheme": "To speak of the Supreme Being in terms of impious irreverence; to revile or speak reproachfully of God, or the Holy Spirit".

What does it mean to speak in terms of "impious irreverence"?

> Impious: 1. Irreverent towards the Supreme Being; wanting in veneration for God and his authority; irreligious; profane.
>
> 2. Irreverent towards God; proceeding from or manifesting a contempt for the Supreme Being; **tending to dishonor God or his laws,** and **bring them into contempt**; as an impious deed; impious language; impious writings.

Jeremiah prophesied of those who pay lip service to the Lord but who dishonor and bring in contempt God's laws:

> "Thus saith the Lord of hosts, hearken not unto the words of the prophets that prophesy unto you: they make you vain: they speak a vision of their own heart, and not out of the mouth of the Lord. They say still unto them that despise me, **The Lord has said Ye shall have peace; and they say unto every one that walketh after the imagination of his own heart, no evil shall come upon you.**" Jeremiah 23:16-17

These prophets which Jeremiah describes are lying. In other words, the Lord is *not* saying to those that despise him "Ye shall have peace," even though the prophets are saying so. The Lord is *not* saying to everyone that walketh after the imagination of his own heart, "No evil shall come upon you," and yet, that is what these prophets which Jeremiah describes declare. Prophets who should be His mouthpiece, but speaking in His name are mouthpieces for vanity instead. One is reminded of powerful voices which affirm and even celebrate those committing crimes, sins, and abuses against their own body .

There is more I intended to write in this chapter, but I discovered the intended material is more appropriate for a separate book. For now, we will confine ourselves to the present discussion.

President Nelson said that the vaccine was a *literal godsend*. Indeed, it may have been, but not in the way RMN meant it. The etymology of the word 'godsend' comes from "God sends" and "message", i.e. God sends a message.[83] When Assyrians took the Northern Kingdom of Israel captive, the Assyrians were a godsend also: "And the Lord rejected all the seed of Israel, and afflicted them, and delivered them into the hand of spoilers, until he had cast them out of his sight" (2 Kings 17: 21, see also the same principle with the kingdom of Judah in 2 Kings 25:2). In 2021 and 2022 the number one cause of death for those who were vaccinated and under the age of 65 was sudden death. This wasn't an issue at all for the same age group who were unvaccinated.[84] If the mouthpiece of the Lord says the vaccine is a "*literal godsend*" then what message is God sending?

---

[83]godsend | Etymology, origin and meaning of godsend by etymonline, https://www.etymonline.com/word/godsend

[84]"My data showed that, among other things, "died suddenly" wasn't an issue at all for those <65 who were unvaccinated in 2021 and 2022. But it was the #1 cause of death for those in that age group who were vaccinated in the same 2021-2022 timeframe" ("Now everyone can easily prove the vax should be stopped", Steve Kirsch, https://stevekirsch.substack.com/p/now-everyone-can-easily-prove-the, 26 Dec 2022. See also The Defender article on the same "The No. 1 Cause of Death for Under 65s in 2021 — Sudden Death", Dr. Joseph Mercola, https://childrenshealthdefense.org/defender/sudden-death-number-one-cause-under-65-covid-vaccine-cola/, 11 Jan 2023.

Chapter 5: Answers to Prayers

In a Sunday school lesson, a teacher desired to reiterate the blessing we had of having President Nelson as a prophet. She asked, "what are things that stand out to you from President Nelson's time as President?" This question was revealing because the question was not aimed at discussing the blessing of having a living prophet, but rather the blessing of RMN as that appointed prophet. The danger of focusing on the man himself is that is it can lead to a cult of personality. This has happened many times in history, one of the most well-known is Germany in the 30s, when judges were instructed that Hitler was the law, and the law was no longer looked for as justification. Instead of the law, Germany's judges looked at the latest speeches and pronouncements from the Fuhrer for their reasoning.[85] George Q. Cannon described a related principle:

> "The Lord designs that the principle of knowledge shall be developed in every heart, that all may stand before Him in the dignity of their manhood, doing understandingly what He requires of them, not depending upon nor being blindly led by their priests or leaders, **as is the universal custom,** *and one of the most fruitful sources of evil to the people on the face of the earth* (emphasis added).[86]

---

[85]"Dr. Hans Frank, Commissioner of Justice and Reich Law Leader, told the jurists in 1936, 'the National Socialist ideology is the foundation of all basic laws, especially as explained in the party program and in the speeches of the Fuehrer... There is no independence of law against National Socialism. Say to yourselves at every decision you make: 'How would the Fuehrer decide in my place?'", quoted in *The Rise and Fall of the Third Reich: A History of Nazi Germany*, p. 268, William L. Shirer, Simon and Schuster 1960.

[86]Cannon, George Q.. Journal of Discourses. Vol. 12. 45. April 21, 1867, quoted in "If Thine Eye Offend The (Part 1 – Blind Obedience? To Question or Not to Question? That is the Question", James F. Stoddard III with L. Hannah Stoddard, Joseph Smith Foundation, https://josephsmithfoundation.org/papers/if-thine-eye-offend-thee-part-1-blind-obedience-to-question-or-not-to-question-that-is-the-question/ accessed 30 Jan 2023.

The answers to that Sunday school question were also revealing. They included two-hour church, the Come Follow Me program (both in motion before RMN's tenure as president), the weeklong social media fast for the youth etc. No one mentioned that which RMN had striven to make the hallmark of his presidency up to that time with two official statements, two worldwide fasts, social media posts, conference talks and wide sweeping masking and vaccination policies—that is, his response to Covid. How could something so prominent of his presidency have escaped the mention of an adoring class? Because like Germany in the 1930's and 40's, certain topics illustrating blindness become taboo.

When President Nelson first asked for a worldwide fast on March 26th, 2020 (for March 29th) little was known about the Covid situation. China was locking people in their houses and broadcasting people dying in the street. In February, the *Daily Mail* and *The Epoch Times* reported Wuhan crematoriums 'are burning bodies 24/7 to cope with extra workload during coronavirus outbreak'.[87] By March 19th news outlets reported 21 million Chinese cell phones dropped in only three months, leading many to consider the death toll in China must be extraordinary.[88] The Lancet published an article days before on March 16th predicting millions dying from COVID in western countries.

With the first fast on March 29th, and the second fast that President Nelson requested on April 4th 2020 (for April 10th) many united in sincere prayer and faith "pleading for relief from this pandemic" and healing "throughout the world".[89] If indeed COVID-19 was

---

[87] "Wuhan crematoriums 'are burning bodies 24/7 to cope with extra workload during coronavirus outbreak'", Sophie Tanno, Daily Mail, https://www.dailymail.co.uk/news/article-7969861/Wuhan-crematoriums-burning-bodies-24-7-cope-extra-workload.html

[88] "21 Million Fewer Cellphone Users in China May Suggest a High CCP Virus Death Toll", Nicole Halo, *The Epoch Times*, https://www.theepochtimes.com/the-closing-of-21-million-cell-phone-accounts-in-china-may-suggest-a-high-ccp-virus-death-toll_3281291.html, 22 Mar 2020, updated 2 April 2020.

[89] "President Nelson calls for a second worldwide fast in response to COVID-19", Jason Swensen, Church News, https://www.thechurchnews.com/2020/4/4/23216121/general-conference-april-2020-worldwide-fast-president-nelson, 4 April 2020.

particularly deadly at this time of year as was suggested by the above referenced material, its level of harm greatly diminished after these fasts. Despite the theatrics presented by the press, Covid became a disease no more dangerous than a typical flu or some colds of other years. The millions of dead predicted did not occur. I believe that the fasting by the general membership of the church as well as the prayers, fasting, and faith of many outside the church may very well have been the cause of the mildness of Covid-19 generally. This could have been the legacy we remembered. Prayers and fasts answered. Unfortunately, like Sampson with Delilah, subsequent actions would overshadow this initial appeal to the Lord as RMN followed this action with an extreme push to support and enforce the pharmaceutical agenda.

Chapter 6: Standing Before God

Despite the resultant mildness of Covid-19 conditions, the global vaccine caucus sought to use Covid-19 as a means of power and wealth accumulation. The narrative of emergency and of the lie of no available therapeutics continued to ensure "Emergency Use Authorization" was met for the vaccine roll out. RMN, true to promises made to the G20 in October of 2020 did his best to get members of the church to take the vaccine despite any misgivings they had toward it.

Vaccine uptake was the desire of the global elite who were of a similar collectivist stripe as RMN. Church leadership as high as the area presidency received notice not to allow any belief exemptions against vaccination and that even the doctrine of agency was not to be used as a religious basis to be exempt from the vaccine. Bishops and Stake presidents were threatened that such allowances could be considered perjury. [90] This was particularly hurtful to those in the military, teachers, or medical professionals where vaccines were required. As they attempted to get a religious belief exemption; they were left in the lurch to show how their own religious beliefs were sincere despite their religious leader saying they were invalid. Such actions by church leadership had a flavor of vindictiveness characteristic of many who promoted the vaccine as the only solution to the inconveniences and heartaches of the 'pandemic.' Some were surprised at RMN's authoritarian approach; however, he telegraphed his paradigm in several interviews soon after becoming president of the church as recorded in his biography by Sheri Dew. When asked what he thought

---

[90] LDS Church tells California leaders to not approve religious exemption to COVID-19 vaccine mandates, Spencer Burt. https://www.fox13now.com/news/coronavirus/lds-church-tells-california-leaders-to-not-approve-religious-exemption-to-covid-19-vaccine-mandates

about immigration, the United States was building a border wall. RMN said he "didn't like fences." He expressed that he felt abortion law in the United States was settled and unlikely to reverse (which, however, it did).[91] He also promoted typical socialist talking points after shootings in Florida: "It's natural for you and others to say 'How could God allow things like that to happen?' Well, God allows us to have our agency and men have passed laws that allow guns to go to people who shouldn't have them." As is routine of authoritarian lobbyists, he alluded to gun rights as the problem and cause of the tragedy, rather than the choices of the actual perpetrators of the crime, also ignoring that no matter what laws are passed, evil men will still break laws.[92]

RMN's attitudes are reminiscent of John Dewey's. Ezra Taft Benson warned against this same Dewey,[93] known as the father of modern American education (with its focus on social activities as the center of schooling). In one of the most damning lists of deceiving men, Benson said, "Parents can help expose some of the deceptions of men like Sigmund Freud, Charles Darwin, John Dewey, Karl Marx, John Keynes, and others" (Conference Report Oct 1970).[94] John Dewey said, "You can't make socialists out of individualists. Children who know how to think for themselves spoil the harmony of the collective

---

[91] *Insights From A Prophet's Life: Russell M. Nelson*, Sheri Dew, Deseret Book Company, 2019, p. 427-428.
[92] https://kutv.com/news/nation-world/lds-president-russell-m-nelson-comments-on-the-recent-florida-school-shooting
[93] Dewey was renowned for advancing collectivism. "Dewey wanted to fundamentally transform the United States. He wanted it to look more like the Soviet Union, in fact. To do that, he believed a total transformation of education and society was required—literally "changing the conception of what constitutes education," as he wrote in "The Relation of Theory to Practice in Education" in 1904." ("How John Dewey Used Public 'Education' to Subvert Liberty", Alex Newman, Illinois Family Institute, https://illinoisfamily.org/education/how-john-dewey-used-public-education-to-subvert-liberty/, 13 Mar 2021). See also John Dewey's book *Impressions of Soviet Russia and the Revolutionary World*, where he gushes in admiration of the Soviet System for undermining the family, which Dewey suggested was a 'breeder of non-social interests.' Believing Soviet education exemplary, he said American educators should study the Soviet system, from which they "would learn much more than from any other country" (p. 107-108). https://archive.org/details/impressions_of_soviet_russia/
[94] Also quoted under the heading "President Benson Names 5 Anit-Christs" at the Joseph Smith Foundation, https://josephsmithfoundation.org/anti-christ/.

society which is coming, where everyone is interdependent."[95] In other words, teach children to be "good global citizens" by making them socialists. Given the parallels of John Dewey's attitudes with RMN's, this author suspects RMN studied John Dewey, especially as RMN expresses a socialist approach to global citizenship in the same way that Dewey's writings are drenched. In preparation for this book, this author discovered in the philosophy and paradigm of John Dewey a surprisingly accurate explanation and measuring stick for RMN's attitudes and motivations.[96]

It is obvious RMN disagrees politically with the J. Reuben Clarks, David O. McKays, Ezra Taft Bensons, and Harold B. Lees of church history and leadership. However, when RMN chose to use his mantel of authority to endorse the agenda of the Gadianton robbers of our day and actively promote their goals, he abandoned the arena of ethereal political opinion for actively molding the world into the shape desired by the most wicked. Now when I am asked to show my vote, in favor or opposition of a proposal that RMN remain as president of the church, how can I see myself answering for that vote in front of the Savior? Can I really vote in favor of a proposal to keep President Nelson at the head of the church with a clear conscience? For this author, the answer is no. I cannot. When the choice is placed before me, I cannot support the machinations causing miscarriages, cancer[97],

---

[95] "The NEA Agenda? How John Dewey, Socialism Influenced Public Education", David Fiorazo, https://davidfiorazo.com/2013/02/the-nea-agenda-how-john-deweysocialism-influenced-public-education/, 21 Feb 2013.

[96] The same could probably, and regrettably, be said of much of the American population, as John Dewey's philosophy and paradigm have permeated the American school system (and those patterned after it) for many decades. Insightful books on how the American public school system is used to inculcate these kinds of attitudes include *None Dare Call It Education* by John Stormer (Christian perspective), *Inside American Education* by Thomas Sowell (academic perspective), and the writings of John Taylor Gatto, including *Weapons of Mass Instruction: A Schoolteacher's Journey through the Dark World of Compulsory Schooling* (most recent).

[97] "In late December 2022, Steve Kirsch and Jessica Rose, Ph.D., both published Substack articles detailing some of the latest evidence showing the shots are destroying people's immune systems and have triggered an avalanche of turbo-charged cancers ... So, to summarize the effects in layman's terms, the switch from spike-specific neutralizing IgG antibodies to IgG4 antibodies switches your body from tumor suppression mode into tumor progression mode, as cancerous cells now can evade your immune system" (("The No.

premature death[98] and life altering disabilities of all kinds based on lies, and yet told as truth by the very man whom we uphold as the promulgator of truth. RMN's loyalty appears to be to his own medical legacy, and to maintain solidarity with those that not only promote decreased birth rates and increasing death rates, but who, through promoting death, become enriched. Is not the delivery of the entire membership of the church into the hands of conspiring men seeking to make money over their death an action worthy of opposition? I.E. "Any opposed?"

Moroni warned what we should be looking for in the last days:

"Wherefore, O ye Gentiles, it is wisdom in God that these things should be shown unto you, that thereby ye may repent of your sins, and **suffer not that these murderous combinations shall get above you, which are built up to get power and gain–and the work, yea, even the work of destruction come upon you,**

"**Wherefore, the Lord commandeth you, when ye shall see these things come among you that ye shall awake to a sense of your awful situation, because of this secret combination which shall be among you;** . . .

"For it cometh to pass that **whoso buildeth it up seeketh to overthrow the freedom of all lands, nations and countries;** and it bringeth to pass the destruction of all people, for it is built up by the devil, who is the father of all lies; . . ." (Ibid., 8:23-25. Italics added.) Quoted in Ezra Taft Bensons Talk "Secret Combinations" Secret Combinations | Ezra Taft Benson |

---

1 Cause of Death for Under 65s in 2021 — Sudden Death", Dr. Joseph Mercola, The Defender, https://childrenshealthdefense.org/defender/sudden-death-number-one-cause-under-65-covid-vaccine-cola/, 11 Jan 2023.)

[98]"... differences between the jabbed and unjabbed: 1. Sudden death rates are off the charts for the vaccinated cf. unvaccinated for those <65. ... It's the #1 cause of death for this age group ... 2. Myocarditis as a cause of death is registering now for both age ranges but only for the vaccinated. ... 3. Cardiac issues as a cause of death in vaccinated young people (<65) are significantly elevated vs. their unvaxxed peers" (ibid).

American Heritage of Freedom (latterdayconservative.com). https://www.latterdayconservative.com/ezra-taft-benson/secret-combinations/

In response to Moroni's warning we should be actively aware and on the lookout for these secret combinations. The associations and unions and groups we are looking for are murderous, they are built up for power and gain, and they are secret, in other words, they strive to keep their operations "hid, concealed from the notice or knowledge of all persons" (1828 dictionary 'secret').

Case in point. The FDA sought to conceal its data on the vaccines for 75 years.[99]

The plandemic was based on murderous intent. The vaccine in particular is murderous, increasing premature death, increasing infertility, increasing miscarriages. It is a depopulation bomb unleashed on the planet. While furthering depopulation goals, it enriched those behind the vaccine, many receiving royalties outside of the public eye, and garnering power to the power hungry. When we look back at this time, we will recognize, that this was World War III,[100] but this time it was nearly every government at war with their own population.[101]

Can we, with a clear conscience vote in favor of man who is supporting these secret combinations? Can we trust his loyalty to church members is greater than his loyalty to his peers in the secret

---

[99]"FDA Says It Now Needs 75 Years to Fully Release Pfizer COVID-19 Vaccine Data", Zachary Stieber, The Epoch Times, https://www.allsides.com/news/2021-12-08-1553/fda-says-it-now-needs-75-years-fully-release-pfizer-covid-19-vaccine-data 8 Dec 2021.

[100]"The scale of socio-economic disruption seen under Covid has only ever been witnessed in times of war." Hughes, Kyrie & Broudy from "Covid -19 Mass Formation or Mass Atrocity", *Unlimited Hangout*, 29 Nov 2022.

[101]"We are facing an intentional effort to poison people. One of the things you learn when you're a government official in Washington is, if something continues to go on after it's been proven to be not effective, that's when you realize the real goal is what's happening as opposed to the stated goal…What we are looking at is mass murder." Catherine Austin Fitts, former U.S. Assistant Secretary of Housing and Urban Development for Housing. From "Doctors for Covid Ethics Symposium 5, 3:45:09-3:45:28. 10 Dec 2022. https://rumble.com/v1zzehm-doctors-for-covid-ethics-symposium-5.html See also the David Hughes video at 4:50:37-5:31:10 of the same link.

societies of Skull and Bones and the Owl and Key (that he himself was proud to announce his affiliation with in his autobiography)[102] of which many other collectivist elites belong?[103] What will be the next agenda for which the lives of church members are promised as dividends?

Unlike the ballot to vote for political elections, everyone at stake and ward conference will see a dissenting vote to a proposal for the First Presidency. Is the public nature of that vote sufficient reason to hide? Who are we more afraid of, God or man? Even before stake conference, those who vote against any of the proposals proposed at General Conference are asked to speak with their stake president. Is not the concern that as a church we are furthering the agenda of the Gadianton Robbers of our day worth a conversation with the Stake President? Is it so hard a thing to stand up and be counted?

In New Testament times, the religious elite lost their way, currying political favors and power. In Old Testament times as well, the religious elite also lost their way in flattering the people in their sins. Is it such a surprise that in our day we should be tested on where our faith is really founded? Is our faith founded on a man? A system? Or on Christ?

We referred to the story of the man of God in 1 Kings 13. The JST of 1 Kings 13:18 records that the senior prophet said to the man of God "I am a prophet also as thou art; and an angle spake unto me

---

[102] "I was also later elected to honorary societies of Skull and Bones in the junior year, Owl and Key in the Senior year," *From Heart to Heart: An Autobiography of Russell Marion Nelson*, p.48, Russell Marion Nelson, Quality Press, 1979. Also cited in Chapter 4 of Spencer Condie's *Russell M. Nelson: Father, Surgeon, Apostle*. "He was subsequently elected to several other honorary scholastic societies, including Skull and Bones, Owl and Key...." p.47 Kindle version. Finally, watch "Church Leaders and Skull and Bones," Ben McClintock, Tree of Liberty Society 21 Nov 2022, minutes 13:45 to 14:55 of https://treeoflibertysociety.com/skull-bones-and-church-leaders/

[103] "Deep State Secret Societies: Skull & Bones, Bohemians, Illuminati", Alex Newman, The New American, 2 Nov 2017, https://thenewamerican.com/deep-state-secret-societies-skull-bones-bohemians-illuminati/; See also *America's Secret Establishment: An Introduction to the Order of Skull & Bones*, Anthony C. Sutton, Trine Day 2004. See also *How the Order Controls Education*, Anthony Sutton, Veritas, 1985. See also "Conspiracies Old and New", Sam Blumenfeld, The New American, 14 Dec 2011, https://thenewamerican.com/conspiracies-old-and-new/; also "What is Skull and Bones, Ben McClintock, Tree of Liberty Society 26 Dec 2022, https://treeoflibertysociety.com/what-is-the-skull-bones-society/.

by the word of the Lord, saying, Bring him back with thee into thine house, that he may eat bread and drink water, *that I may prove him; and he* lied *not* unto him".

The Lord desired to test the man of God. Was he loyal to God? Or did he fear a prophet more than God? How are we doing in proving to the Lord who we are loyal to?

Joseph Smith once said, "I don't blame anyone for not believing my history; if I had not experienced what I have I could not have believed it myself."[104] I likewise blame no person for not opposing RMN at each proposal for his continued administration. Hopefully, however, for those who still choose to vote in favor of him, perhaps this book will encourage understanding and acceptance for those that choose to oppose. Like a testimony of the Book of Mormon, a witness of the truth regarding one's own life and the evils that we are up against must be discovered. Both are not made plain except to those who search for truth.

President J. Reuben Clark taught, "With this view of the rights, powers, and duties of the President of the High Priesthood of the Church, and also of the First Presidency, it is clear that the sustaining vote by the people is not, and is not to be regarded as, a mere matter of form, but on the contrary *a matter of the* **last** *gravity*. Every person is **entitled** to indicate whether or not he or she can sustain the officer proposed" (emphasis added).[105] The Lord himself established the pattern and responsibility of such a vote, instructing the saints, "And a commandment I give unto you, that you should fill all these offices and approve of those names which I have mentioned, **or else disapprove of them at my general conference**" (D&C 124:144). **The Lord has put approval** *and disapproval* **of proposed church officers within the purview** *and stewardship* **of the general membership of the church.**

[104]"History, 1838–1856, volume E-1 [1 July 1843–30 April 1844]," p. 1979, The Joseph Smith Papers, accessed March 22, 2023, https://www.josephsmithpapers.org/paper-summary/history-1838-1856-volume-e-1-1-july-1843-30-april-1844/351.

[105]President J. Reuben Clark Jr., Conference Report April 1940, p. 73-74. https://archive.org/details/conferencereport1940a/page/n73/mode/2up

As this book neared publication I came across an article titled "Respect for our Leaders." It masterfully discusses Christ's teachings on the matter, particularly from JST Mark Chapter 9, and the lessons we have learned on this topic in history. I highly recommend every member of the church reading this book to also consult that article from which this quote was taken:

> Being "appointed" [from JST Mark 9:46] clearly infers priesthood authority. He has not called himself. He has not been selected by democratic vote. He has been called by God to lead, to assist the weak, to watch over the flock and bring the light of God to a darkened world. His high position may lead us to conclude that he could not fall. Would the Lord appoint a man who later becomes a "transgressor"? The Lord has indicated that He could. What should our reaction be? According to God, we must "pluck him out" as our stewardship permits.[106]

The question of whether a prophet, so appointed, could become a transgressor is answered by Abinadi in Mosiah 15:13, where he specifically excludes prophets who have fallen into transgression from the other prophets he describes. Our stewardship, as members of the church permits us (perhaps even demands us, depending on our situation) to vote "oppose" when the sustaining of church officers is proposed. President Clark defined what should happen: "Anyone not desiring to sustain anyone proposed may not only indicate his dissent here but he may, if he wishes, present his objections to the proper authority of the Church, and will be given an appropriate hearing. This is the rule and order of the Church."[107]

---

[106] "If Thine Eye Offend The (Part 1 – Blind Obedience? To Question or Not to Question? That is the Question", James F. Stoddard III with L. Hannah Stoddard, Joseph Smith Foundation, https://josephsmithfoundation.org/papers/if-thine-eye-offend-thee-part-1-blind-obedience-to-question-or-not-to-question-that-is-the-question/ accessed 30 Jan 2023.

[107] President J. Reuben Clark Jr., Conference Report April 1940, p. 72. https://archive.org/details/conferencereport1940a/page/n73/mode/2up

In the end, the Lord will win. From the prophecy of Isaiah 9:13-16, both the ancient and the prophet who teaches lies are cut off. Some prophecies such as these are fulfilled multiple times, and yet the Lord's works moves forward. Our own influence in the church can and should be felt. We must awaken to an awful sense of our situation and not let the secret combinations of our day get above us. If they are above us in the government, let us make that known and tear them down. If they are above us in the church, let us humbly manifest that as our stewardship permits, and in so doing, call down the blessings of heaven for having passed the test of proving our loyalty to God over man.

In the words of Ezra Taft Benson:

Have we, as Moroni warned, "polluted the holy church of God?" (Morm. 8:38.)

"My people are destroyed for lack of knowledge," lamented Hosea. (Hos. 4:6.) Today, because some parents have refused to become informed and then stand up and inform their children, they are witnessing the gradual physical and spiritual destruction of their posterity. If we would become like God, knowing good and evil, then we had best find out what is undermining us, how to avoid it, and what we can do about it. (General Conference, 1970)[108]

---

[108] https://josephsmithfoundation.org/docs/a-plea-to-strengthen-our-families/.

Chapter 7: Standing for Truth

Christ has many names. The Messiah, The Christ, The Savior of Mankind, Jesus, Lord, Jehovah, Lord of Hosts, Redeemer, King of Kings, the great I AM, the Holy One, the Eternal Judge, the Eternal God. Before any of these was his name, key to the war in Heaven, he was *the Firstborn*. In that capacity, he led all loyal to the Father during the war in Heaven. All of us who came to Earth at some point joined with him, thereby keeping our first estate and maintaining the opportunity to come to Earth and be born with a mortal body.

The war in Heaven was about choice. Defending the Father's plan to preserve the agency of man. The adversary, on the other hand, pursued a plan on behalf of the collective. All, he claimed, would return home, under his tyrannical rule.

The war in Heaven continues on Earth, and those that are still loyal to *the Firstborn* defend what *He* defended on Earth, just as they did in pre-mortal Heaven. David O. McKay said:

> I come with another theme this morning-**Two Contending Forces**. Those forces are known and have been designated by different terms throughout the ages. "In the beginning," they were known as Satan on the one hand and Christ on the other.
>
> In Joshua's time, they were called "gods of the Amorites" for one and "the Lord" for the other. Paul spoke of "the works of the flesh" on the one hand and "fruits of the spirit" on the other. They are often spoken of as "selfishness" for one, "life of service," the other. **In these days, they are called "domination**

by the state" on the one hand, "personal liberty" on the other, communism[109] on the one hand, and free agency on the other.

As a text, I say to you, "Choose you this day whom ye will serve." (Josh. 24:15.) (Emphasis added, (David O. McKay. Two Contending Forces. May 18, 1960.) [110]

Those so engaged in defending freedom and liberty, choosing to serve the Lord and stand with the Lord, even when they may not remember his name or are ignorant of the divinely ordained role standing for and defending liberty has in this life, they will nevertheless, know Him when they see Him, for He will stand for all the good and righteousness that they remember and which rings in their souls like a clarion call.

Ezra Taft Benson further explained:

The central issue in the premortal council was: Shall the children of God have untrammeled agency to choose the course they should follow, whether good or evil or shall they be coerced and forced to be obedient? Christ and all who followed him stood for the former proposition-freedom of choice; Satan stood for the latte—coercion and force. The war that began in Heaven over this issue is not yet over. The conflict continues on the battlefield of mortality. And **one of Lucifer's primary strategies has**

---

109 Shockingly enough, communism also figured prominently in the forces that supported the Covid-19 vaccine agenda: "Every global predator we could identify is financially wedded to and filled with admiration for, not the United States or other Western democracies, but for Communist China and totalitarianism…This menacing group includes most of the world's billionaires and major institutions of the West, and it is backed by the Chinese Communist Party." (emphasis original). *COVID-19 and the Global Predators: We Are the Prey*. Peter Breggin, Ginger Breggin. Preface. Nov 2021. Lake Edge Press.

110 Text of President McKay's talk here: https://www.latterdayconservative.com/education/a-course-on-liberty/the-war-in-heaven-on-earth-today/?fbclid=IwAR2LfIiUfjaWK-mj5f54tUEndnAE_v69OdrXufMS98bIgU-PVENPHO8yCN_Y, **audio available here:** https://speeches.byu.edu/talks/david-o-mckay/two-contending-forces/

been to restrict our agency through the power of earthly governments. (The Constitution a Heavenly Banner. Ezra Taft Benson. 16 September 1986.)[111]

On the other hand, there are many who profess to know His name but who fight against what the Lord fought for as *the Firstborn*. They confederate themselves with those who murder to get gain, who use the force of government to stop the promulgation or even the conversation of seeking for truth; who use the necessities of life and employment to shackle humanity into slavery, attempting to make these necessities available to only those who submit to their diabolical agenda.[112]

Tracy Beanz of UncoverDC described the uniqueness of the Covid-19 assault on liberty:

> "The U.S. Government, guided by the CDC, NIH, and other bureaucracies, literally DESTROYED the entire country. And it wasn't just a United States thing; it was an entire world thing. It was tyrannical globalism. Not the kind that is ushered in by getting folks all amped up about global warming. This was much different. ***This was forced***."[113] (emphasis added).

This is a clear modern description of what Moroni prophesied, "that whoso buildeth it up seeketh to overthrow the freedom of all lands, nations, and countries" (Ether 8: 25). In such situations, as many

---

[111] For further information on this topic, see "The War in Heaven on Earth Today" at https://www.latterdayconservative.com/education/a-course-on-liberty/the-war-in-heaven-on-earth-today/?fbclid=IwAR3dOf45Mv7aHW4b_N2ICzY-HwHkxpAIYMdP67nEvIfGZykhQAGNc3ZZNkzY.

[112] As published by Whitney Webb and *Unlimited Hangout*, "Thus, by exploiting the human needs for physical and social survival a war is born … carefully imposed from conception through planning to its incarnation in flesh and blood" Hughes, Kyrie & Broudy "Covid -19 Mass Formation or Mass Atrocity" 29 Nov 2022. https://unlimitedhangout.com/2022/11/investigative-reports/covid-19-mass-formation-or-mass-atrocity/

[113] "A Reckoning Is Coming. Can They Escape It?", Tracy Beanz, UnCoverDC.com, https://www.uncoverdc.com/2022/08/22/a-reckoning-is-coming-can-they-escape-it/ , 22 Aug 2022.

recently learned, non-compliance to tyrants is obedience to God.[114] "Monsters exist, but they are far too few in number in to be truly dangerous; the most dangerous monsters are ordinary [men and women] ready to believe and obey without asking questions" (Primo Levi). The fight for freedom continues to rage. The enemies of truth and liberty will continue to morph and adjust their angle. On the shoulders of the vigilant few, willing to make the first move, even while mocked, misunderstood, inconvenienced, and persecuted, rests the eventual awakening of the majority to the awfulness of our situation.

As an extended epilogue to this book, I recommend the following three videos (in this order) as a preparation for the next assault on freedom that inevitably will come:

- On Rumble: "How Civil Disobedience Safeguards Freedom and Prevents Tyranny (13 min). https://rumble.com/vrlubt-how-civil-disobedience-safeguards-freedom-and-prevents-tyranny.html
    - This video explains the philosophical basis and necessity of the peaceful dissident to prevent tyranny from overcoming any civilization.
- On Vimeo: *Noncompliant Movie,* https://vimeo.com/562959655
    - This video explains the Constitutional right and Christian imperative to stand against unjust laws and Not Comply.
- On BitChute: "Full Film: Must Christians Obey the Government" https://www.bitchute.com/video/814Lo647NDmS/
    - This video continues the logic and understanding of the previous video, discussing the Christian

---

114   Paraphrasing Thomas Jefferson's proposed motto for the United States "Rebellion to tyrants is obedience to God", https://www.monticello.org/research-education/thomas-jefferson-encyclopedia/personal-seal/

obligation to stand for truth, even in face of a corrupt and unjust laws, and continues further with discussing latter-day saint doctrine from the Doctrine and Covenants, Joseph Smith, and other Latter-Day prophets.

Decide who you will be the next time we are assaulted with tyranny and lies. Seek the word of the Lord daily, both in scripture study and prayer. Stand for truth, agency, and all that the Lord has asked us to stand for. This is the endeavor to which Lord has called us. To reiterate Joseph Smith's words previously quoted, "It is our duty to concentrate all our influence to make popular that which is sound and good, and unpopular that which is unsound."[115] President John Taylor said, "Besides the preaching of the Gospel, we have another mission, namely, the perpetuation of the free agency of man and the maintenance of liberty, freedom, and the rights of man."[116] Reiterating the importance of the Constitution, President David O. McKay said, "Next to being one in worshiping God, there is nothing in this world upon which this Church should be more united than in upholding and defending the Constitution of the United States."[117] We are called to stand for truth, for the agency of man, for Christ, and to follow Him, even when it is inconvenient. We are offered the choice, to trust in the arm of flesh, with it's attendant shackels and chains, or take upon us the yoke of Christ, with the peace and joy that fills the hearts of those who know and serve him. Let us choose Christ over man.

---

[115]*History of the Church* 5:286, quoted by Ezra Taft Benson in *This Nation Shall Endure,* 1977. See "America's Home" at Latter-day Conservative, https://www.latterdayconservative.com/ezra-taft-benson/americas-hope/ accessed 30 Jan 2023.
[116]General Conference April 1882. Journal of Discourses 23:63, https://en.wikisource.org/wiki/Journal_of_Discourses/Volume_23/The_Gospel%27s_Restoration,_etc. quoted at https://www.latterdayconservative.com/quote/journal-discourses-23-63/
[117]McKay, David O, "The Enemy Within", 34, quoted at Latter-day Conservative, https://www.latterdayconservative.com/quote/the-enemy-within-34/

Afterward

For Further Study

As stated in the author's note, this book was not meant as an exhaustive catalogue of the fraud and corruption referred to in this book. I suggest the following for further study as a primer and witness to the truth that occurred during the Covid-19 pandemic.

1. Complete steps outlined in Chapter 0 of this book.

2. **Watch the following Episodes of *The Highwire* with Del Bigtree:** the (The HighWire | Watch https://thehighwire.com/watch/?category=archive#watch-explore): 175, 248, 249, 252, 257, 272, 293, 298, 300. Additional: 200, 223, 224, 246, 242, 255, 271, 286, and whatever is the latest episode.

3. **Read *The Real Anthony Fauci*** by Robert F. Kennedy Jr (at least chapters 1,2 and 9,11,12– they are long chapters). The Real Anthony Fauci: Big Pharma's Global War on Democracy, Humanity, and Public Health • Children's Health Defense (childrenshealthdefense.org) https://childrenshealthdefense.org/store/the-real-anthony-fauci-big-pharmas-global-war-on-democracy-humanity-and-public-health/

4. **Read "*Cause Unknown": The Epidemic of Sudden Deaths in 2021 and 2022*** by Ed Dowd. "Cause Unknown": The Epidemic of Sudden Deaths in 2021 & 2022 (Children's Health Defense): Dowd, Ed, de Becker, Gavin, Kennedy Jr., Robert F.: 9781510776395: Amazon.com: Books

5. **Study the work of Dr. Sheri Tenpenny, Dr. Joseph Mercola, Robert Scott Bell and *The Truth About Vaccines* by Ty and Charlene Bollinger** (The Truth About Vaccines | Are Vaccines Safe? | Vaccine Facts https://thetruthaboutvaccines.com/) and http://www.robertscottbell.com/.

6. **Read *The War On Ivermectin: The Medine That Saved Millions and Could Have Ended the COVID Pandemic* by Dr. Pierre Kory.** https://www.amazon.com/War-Ivermectin-Medicine-Millions-Pandemic/dp/151077386X/

7. **Watch *Critical Thinking with Dr. T and Dr. P* and *Critical Thinking with the 5 Docs*.** Odyssey channel here: https://odysee.com/@CriticallyThinking:3

    Especially Episode 73 https://odysee.com/@CriticallyThinking:3/Critically_Thinking_with_Dr_T_and_Dr_P_Episode_73_Sp_Guest_Dr_N:e

8. **Read** the landmark article that helped many realize how much information was available showing zwhy the vaccine should not be trusted as early as April 15, 2021. **"18 Reasons I Won't Be Getting a COVID Vaccine",** Christine Elliot, https://childrenshealthdefense.org/defender/reasons-not-getting-covid-vaccine/

9. **Review** the myriad of articles archived on Covid-19 at these two websites for further study on specific topics:

    a. vaccine - Liberty Counsel Action (lcaction.org) https://lcaction.org/vaccine

    b. COVIDTRUTH | Tommunds.com https://www.tommunds.com/covidtruth

10. **Watch the "Doctors for Covid Ethcis Symposium"** available here: https://home.solari.com/doctors-for-covid-ehtics-symposium-live-stream-december-10th-on-uk-column-

and-chd-tv/ and here: https://doctors4covidethics.org/gold-standard-covid-science-in-practice-an-interdisciplinary-symposium-v-in-the-midst-of-darkness-light-prevails/

11. **Watch the Five-Part Docuseries:** ***Never Again Is Now Global,*** from Holocaust survivor Vera Sharav. Available here: https://ahrp.org/naing-premier/ and here: https://neveragainisnowglobal.com/

The above is but a sampling of the myriad of academic and scientific voices from around the world that were ignored and often actively silenced to protect the official Covid-19 and vaccine narrative.

As mentioned in the body of this book, I recommend the following essay in addition to two others in pursuing a greater understanding of our responsibility as members of the Church in sustaining our church leaders:

1. "If Thine Eye Offend Thee" (Part1 – Blind Obedience – To Question or Not Question? That is the Question!), https://josephsmithfoundation.org/papers/if-thine-eye-offend-thee-part-1-blind-obedience-to-question-or-not-to-question-that-is-the-question/

2. "10 Largely Forgotten, but Timeless Principles, in Sustaining Leaders", https://josephsmithfoundation.org/10-largely-forgotten-but-timeless-principles-in-sustaining-leaders/

3. "Fact-Checking Misquoted Statement on Blindly Following the Prophet," https://josephsmithfoundation.org/fact-checking-misquoted-statements-on-blindly-following-the-prophet/

For an insightful movie (fictional) portraying the role of secret societies and elites who become part of them:

The Brotherhood of the Bell, Directed by Paul Wendkos, was a made for a TV movie in 1970.

For a powerful documentary on standing for the truth, watch the true story of the young Helmuth Hubner, who gave his life standing against the propaganda of the Nazi's[118]:

Helmuth Hubener Story - Joseph Smith Foundation https://www.youtube.com/watch?v=QnOq4gXUJJQ&list=PLN4UzcYI0bdlv3hC-juyzp9n08VhnJ9Dn

Questions, comments, or helpful information can be directed to Palmyra1820@proton.me

---

[118] A full series on this story is in development at the time of this writing: Updates available here: https://www.youtube.com/watch?v=QnOq4gXUJJQ&list=PLN4UzcYI0bdlv3hC-juyzp9n08VhnJ9Dn

Appendix 1

RMN's initial Twitter Post advertising the vaccine:

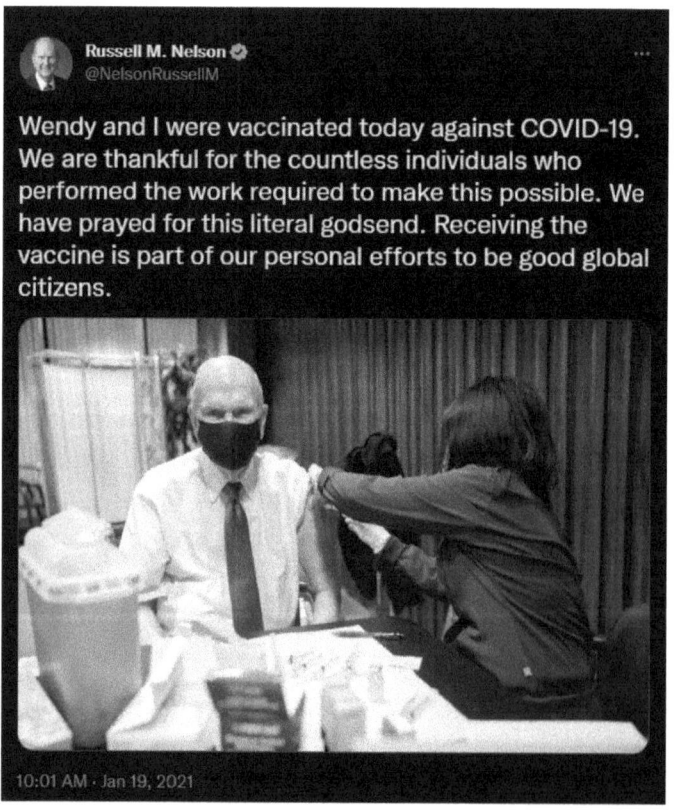

"Wendy and I were vaccinated today against COVID-19. We are thankful for the countless individuals who performed the work required to make this possible. We have prayed for this literal godsend. Receiving the vaccine is part of our personal efforts to be good global citizens."

Keeping his vaccination efforts "personal" was short-lived.

On the same day, the First Presidency released the official statement making their position very un-personal:

"As appropriate opportunities become available, the Church urges its members, employees, and missionaries to be good global citizens and help quell the pandemic by safeguarding themselves and others through immunization."[119]

Missionaries were "encouraged" in April to get the vaccine, with an effective date of August 2021, where any missionary without the COVID-19 vaccine would not be allowed to travel outside their home country. In August of 2021, the First Presidency letter declared the vaccine "safe and effective" and the "only" way to achieve protection from the diseases of Covid-19 and variants, asking all members, from his position as President of the Church, to get the vaccine. In October 2021, President Eyring unabashedly announced at the beginning of the conference that all participating choir members were vaccinated against Covid-19. This was confirmed as a requirement for choir members to perform.

As a literal godsend, Russell M. Nelson may have been correct, but not all godsends are blessings.

"And the Lord sent against him the Chaldees, and bands of Syrians, and the bands of the Moabites, and the bands of the children of Ammon, and sent them against Juda to destroy it, according to the word of the Lord, which he spake by his servants the prophets" (2 Kings 25:2).

---

[119] News Room Release of the Church, 19 Jan 2021, Salt Lake City. At the time of this writing, this News Release was deleted from the newsroom.churchofjesuschristof.org website chronological listing. It can only be found with a direct link here: The First Presidency and Apostles Over Age 70 Receive the COVID-19 Vaccine (churchofjesuschrist.org) https://newsroom.churchofjesuschrist.org/article/church-leaders-covid-19-vaccine.

"We warn that individuals who violate covenants of chastity, who abuse spouse or offspring, or who fail to fulfill family responsibilities will one day stand accountable before God. Further, we warn that the disintegration of the family will bring upon individuals, communities, and nations the calamities foretold by ancient and modern prophets."
– The Family Proclamation, Sept 23, 1995.

Appendix 2

Initial personal study of the First Presidency Letter, written Sept 2021. The information mentioned here was available at the time of the First Presidency message.

The First Presidency of The Church of Jesus Christ of Latter-day Saints sent the following message on Thursday, August 12, 2021, to Church members around the world[120]:

Dear Brothers and Sisters:

We find ourselves fighting a war against the ravages of COVID-19

"ravages" is misleading. We are still at or below normal death rates on a per-annum basis [through the end of 2020].

And its variants.

CDC has admitted they are not testing for variants. Individual hospitals are just saying what variant they think it is without proof or an isolate.

An unrelenting pandemic.

The definition of pandemic recently changed to not include death. The pandemic is very relenting when treatments are made available to people, especially Ivermectin, Budesonide, and Hydroxychloroquine. Look at India. These are very effective. Now, look at the UK and Israel – the pandemic is only unrelenting where the shots are given heavily.

---

120 https://newsroom.churchofjesuschrist.org/article/first-presidency-message-covid-19-august-2021?filter=leadership?filter=leadership

We want to do all we can to limit the spread of these viruses.

That is either untrue or incredibly ignorant. If that were true, they would be promoting proven treatments and habits that promote health: vitamin D, Ivermectin, Hydroxychloroquine, and Budesonide, as well as eating right (78% of those that die from COVID are obese) and encourage people not to wear masks (85% of people who report to the hospital self-identify as wearing masks all the time or almost all the time – according to the CDCs own data).

We know that protection from the diseases they cause can only be achieved by immunizing a very high percentage of the population.

This statement is already proven false by those populations who already have given the shot to a high percentage of the population. The populations with very high vaccination rates have a resurgence in the virus: Israel, the UK, Chile, Portugal, and Spain. India basically had no COVID at all until the vaccination campaign started, and immediately they had a huge spike in cases. It went back down after they started using Ivermectin. Vaccination increases the vulnerability and spread of this virus and attendant diseases.

To limit exposure to these viruses, we urge the use of face masks in public meetings whenever social distancing is not possible.

The use of face masks increases exposure to the virus. Masks and even social distancing are completely useless for aerosols, where particles are suspended for hours or days. Refer to my professional review of face masks.

To provide personal protection from such severe infections, we urge individuals to be vaccinated.

Vaccinations were never even tested against 'severe' infections. Only effective in reducing 'mild symptoms. Does not limit transmission and increases other severe reactions. In addition, Dr. Malone, who invented the mRNA technology, said that currently, the vaccinated are the actual super spreaders because of the reduction of mild symptoms. They won't stay home when they are sick, whereas the unvaccinated will be inclined to stay home at the onset of mild symptoms.

Available vaccines have proven to be both safe and effective.

Untrue. There is no "proof" these are safe and effective. Normal studies for safety were commuted (particularly animal studies). Studies were shortened, and data was not disclosed. Nor have they been effective to stop death or transmission. They only even claim to reduce mild symptoms. This statement is a flat-out lie. Finally, the rate of death in hospitals is much higher for vaccinated than unvaccinated. In addition, miscarriages increased from about 3/10 to 8/10 in pregnant mothers when they received the vaccine in the first trimester.

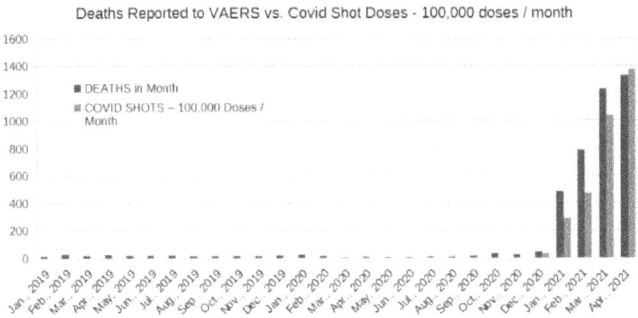

[121]

We can win this war if everyone will follow the wise and thoughtful recommendations of medical experts and government leaders.

Any government leader or medical expert who is encouraging the uptake of these vaccines is neither wise nor thoughtful in the loving sense. They are encouraging a depopulation agenda, seeking the interests of those who developed the patents for this before there was a 'pandemic' and promoting the agenda that the most evil and vile of our world are promoting: Bill Gates, the CCP, Fauci, depolpulationists like Boris Johnson's father, etc.

https://plandemicseries.com/

1hr and 16min documentary "Indoctrination."

Please know of our sincere love and great concern for all of God's children.

---

[121] This graph from TheHighWire.com

Love and concern are not expressed in the persecution of the meek who guard their body as a temple and refuse to intake the devilish and damaging concoctions of those who care nothing for the sanctity of human life.

The First Presidency

Russell M. Nelson

Dallin H. Oaks

Henry B. Eyring

Appendix 3

All Cause Mortality Rates in Vaccinated vs. Unvaccinated (Australia).

Refer to linked pdf below for graphs of all age groups showing similar trends:

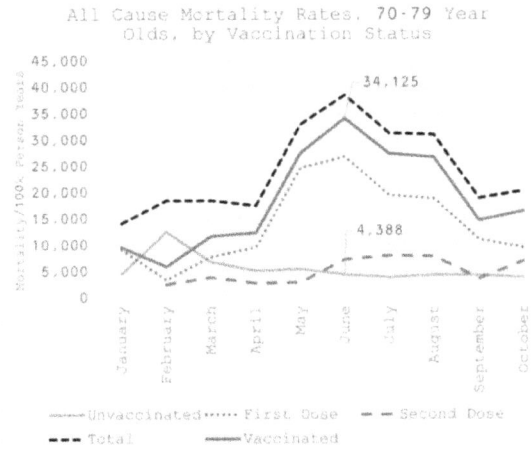

5: All-Cause Mortality 1 January to 31 October 2021 ages 70–79 years: Rate of Death up to 7.8 times higher in Vaccinated versus Unvaccinated.

From Altman et al. 'Letter to Atagi, TGA and Federal Health Minister'. 8th March, 2022. p. 23.

https://www.covidmedicalnetwork.com/open-letters/Letter-to-ATAGI-TGA-FedHealth-8MarchFINALsignatures2.pdf

www.ingramcontent.com/pod-product-compliance
Lightning Source LLC
Chambersburg PA
CBHW041148110526
44590CB00027B/4163